CURSED IN
PENNSYLVANIA

CURSED IN PENNSYLVANIA

STORIES OF THE DAMNED IN THE KEYSTONE STATE

Mark Nesbitt and Patty A. Wilson

Globe
Pequot
GUILFORD, CONNECTICUT

Globe
Pequot

An imprint of Rowman & Littlefield

Distributed by NATIONAL BOOK NETWORK

Copyright © 2016 Mark Nesbitt and Patty A. Wilson

British Library Cataloguing in Publication Information Available

Library of Congress Cataloging-in-Publication Data

Names: Nesbitt, Mark, author.
Title: Cursed in Pennsylvania : stories of the damned in the keystone state /
    Mark Nesbitt and Patty A. Wilson.
Description: Guilford, Connecticut : Globe Pequot, An imprint of Rowman &
    Littlefield, 2016. | Includes bibliographical references and index.
Identifiers: LCCN 2016006028 (print) | LCCN 2016013130 (ebook) | ISBN
    9781493019427 (pbk.) | ISBN 9781493019434 0
Subjects: LCSH: Ghosts—Pennsylvania. | Haunted places—Pennsylvania.
Classification: LCC BF1472.U6 N4625 2016 (print) | LCC BF1472.U6 (ebook) |
    DDC 133.109748—dc23
LC record available at http://lccn.loc.gov/2016006028

♾™ The paper used in this publication meets the minimum requirements of American National Standard for Information Sciences—Permanence of Paper for Printed Library Materials, ANSI/NISO Z39.48-1992.

CONTENTS

PREFACE

Curses! They are something people from the distant past feared. They are the stuff of folklore and religion. They surely cannot hurt us in our modern world. We have electric lights and digital phones. We make sense of the world and view it from afar via our laptops and our televisions. We do not believe in curses, and yet the fear of curses has never gone away. This book is a collection of stories about cursed places, cursed people, and cursed circumstances.

Curses are fueled by hatred, jealousy, anger, greed, and fear. Curses can be deliberately placed upon us through the imprecations of others. Curses can, likewise, be placed upon us by ourselves. Inadvertently, people often put themselves in harm's way. In this book we chose to tell the stories of people who were cursed, of places that were cursed, and of situations where surely a curse was in play.

Curses happened long ago, and those stories are within this book. But even today, there are people who are being cursed. The stories of these modern curses, too, have been included in this volume. Some of the stories came through painstaking research and documentation. Some of the stories were built upon personal interviews with those who were cursed.

It is hard to say what actually makes a curse work. Surely it requires more than unkind words and hateful actions. But it does not seem necessary to perform a ritual in order for a curse to work. There is some invisible line between hateful thoughts and deeds and a curse. Perhaps no one truly knows how curses fall upon us, but there seems little doubt that they do.

Tell the world that you do not believe in curses because they are not rational. Tell yourself that such things surely cannot exist. Whisper to your children that curses are a myth. But still, in some dark corner of your heart, the stories from this book will whisper otherwise. And remember this from author Louis Sachar (*Holes*): "A lot of people don't believe in curses. A lot of people don't believe in yellow-spotted lizards either, but if one bites you, it doesn't make a difference whether you believe in it or not."

INTRODUCTION

The story of Pennsylvania begins as a story of religious freedom. At the age of twenty-two, William Penn, son of a British naval hero, found the Religious Society of Friends (the Quakers), a match for his rebellious nature and his dislike for the fetters of the strict Anglican Church. For his beliefs he would go against his own father as well as the leaders of British society—as far as being jailed in the Tower of London in pursuit of his independence.

He became friends with George Fox, the founder of the Quaker movement, and traveled to Ireland and Germany, witnessing other oppressed minority religions. He was in and out of jail for his written religious tracts and back and forth to Germany and Holland, proselytizing for the Friends. By 1677 he was involved in a group purchasing a tract of land in America—what is presently west New Jersey—to which persecuted Quakers could move.

With that foothold in place, Penn called in a debt King Charles II owed his father, Admiral Sir William Penn, for his support in regaining the throne. Glad to accelerate the departure of the pesky Quakers, Charles granted William Penn the younger forty-five thousand acres of land in America for his mass migration of Quakers. On March 4, 1681, the king signed the charter for the vast wooded land north of Lord Baltimore's Maryland. William Penn named the tract Pennsylvania—"Penn's Woods"—in honor of his father.

Not only were Quakers welcomed to Pennsylvania, but other Protestant Christian sects persecuted by European intolerance. Penn reached out to the Native Americans, signing a treaty after asking permission to "enjoy the land with your love and consent so that we may always live together as neighbors and friends." He established the Friends public school, to become the Philadelphia Public School system in 1689. His independent ideas on democracy were also incorporated in the establishment of Pennsylvania's government. He died in 1718 in England, having created what would later be dubbed "the Keystone State" for its vital importance in holding together the thirteen colonies.

Pennsylvania would be a major battleground during the French and Indian War and would give at least one young American his initial taste of battle. George Washington first went to Erie as an ambassador for the English with the French and Indians. He helped construct Fort Necessity near present-day Pittsburgh, which he later had to surrender. In 1755 he was serving as an aide to British general Edward Braddock when the general was killed at the Battle of the Monongahela, about ten miles east of what became Pittsburgh. As colonel of the Virginia Regiment, Washington fought off French and Indian raids and helped force the surrender of Fort Duquesne. Though he later resigned from his militia post, the fighting he did in Pennsylvania gave him valuable insights into the ways of the British military and provided firsthand experience under fire, something he would use years later to help win his fledgling country's independence from Great Britain.

During the Revolution eastern Pennsylvania became key, as Philadelphia was the largest city in the colonies. As with the rest of America, Pennsylvanians were torn between the centuries-old ties with Great Britain and the movement toward independence. Some had business ties with England; others wished to maintain their loyalty to the king. The Quakers and other religious sects refused to help either side on moral grounds.

The British captured Philadelphia in September 1777, and the city and its environs became the seat of war. George Washington, commander of some 14,600 Continental troops, chose to oppose the British, commanded by General Sir William Howe, along Brandywine Creek. The British victory was costly to the Americans, who left some 1,300 casualties on the battlefield. The colonial defeat also left Philadelphia open for occupation by the British.

At the beginning of October, Washington attacked the British at Germantown. It was another defeat, and the Continentals went into camp at Whitemarsh. Though Washington lost two major battles and the city of Philadelphia, these engagements occupied Howe's army so that it could not bolster British forces at Saratoga in New York, precipitating their surrender to the Americans. The news gained attention from the French, who eventually threw in with the Americans, adding tremendous assistance and support to the cause of independence.

Then there was the Pennsylvania winter of 1777–78. The history of the heroes of Valley Forge is etched into the hearts of all freedom-loving Americans. Their ordeal outside Philadelphia helped galvanize their devotion to the cause of liberty, as it has helped American soldiers endure their own trials ever since.

"Four score and seven years" after those battles for independence, another great battle was fought on Pennsylvania soil in the fields and streets of Gettysburg during the Civil War.

The second Confederate invasion of the north was blunted and turned back by Union troops converging on the crossroads town in south-central Pennsylvania. The accidental initial clash on the morning of July 1, 1863, exploded into the largest battle ever recorded on the North American continent. Ninety-five thousand Union troops fought 75,000 Confederates and left 51,000 casualties lying in the fields and throughout the town to be cared for by a handful of army doctors and orderlies and the 2,400 citizens of Gettysburg. Four months later President Abraham Lincoln came to Gettysburg and delivered an address, two minutes in duration, dedicating the new National Cemetery at Gettysburg, and rededicating the nation to the unfinished business of creating a "new birth of freedom."

In retrospect the Battle of Gettysburg was the watershed for the war. After it the fortunes of the Confederacy receded, their dreams of an independent nation died, and the Union was saved. As one historian put it: "The Union was created in Philadelphia, but it was preserved at Gettysburg."

After the Civil War, Pennsylvania's future lay in industry. Iron, coal, steel, and railroads dominated the economy of the Keystone State and gave jobs and built fortunes for the barons of industry. Science was seeded and watered by the needs of industry; its growth went hand in hand with bringing to the world iron bridges, T-rails for steam locomotives, and Westinghouse's air brakes to stop them.

In Pittsburgh, Charles Hall developed a new metal—aluminum—that would prove essential in winning World War II. Why shouldn't Pennsylvania be central to science in America? One of America's first scientists called it home: Benjamin Franklin.

A trip through one of the many wayside antiques shops in Pennsylvania will allow the collector to pick up a piece that demonstrates why the Commonwealth was called "the Breadbasket of America." From hand-cranked apple peelers, wooden pitchforks, and butter churns to steam-powered tractors, threshers, harvesters, and balers parked out back, one can take a tangible journey through the agricultural history of the Keystone State.

During World War II one-third of the nation's steel came from Bethlehem Steel and its subsidiaries. The Philadelphia Naval Shipyard built fifty-three ships, including the battleships *New Jersey* and *Wisconsin,* and produced warbirds at the Naval Aircraft Factory. Pennsylvania refineries produced the 100-octane aircraft fuel to keep them flying. Pennsylvanians who rose to the rank of general included George C. Marshall, Henry "Hap" Arnold, and Carl Spaatz. Pennsylvania veterans who served in the Twenty-Eighth Infantry Division took a grim pride in their red keystone patch, calling it "the Bloody Bucket."

Pennsylvania will grow on you. You can live the country life or in the big city. You can hike the famous, forested Appalachian Trail, which crosses Pennsylvania, and walk the very heart of the state. You can enjoy the mountains throughout the Commonwealth, roam land over which Union and Confederate troops fought in Gettysburg or where their predecessors suffered at Valley Forge. You can enjoy the hospitality and friendship of its gracious people and glory in its history. But always in your mind are those forbidding, friendly, wild, welcoming woods—"Penn's Woods"—Penns-sylvania.

1

A REVERSE CURSE

Ghost stories swirl about the battlefield of Gettysburg like the apparitions themselves. Where do they come from?

Author Mark Nesbitt has collected well over one thousand ghost stories about the battlefield, the town, and its environs. Many are published in his seven-volume series *Ghosts of Gettysburg*. Still others reside in his file cabinets, waiting to be published.

While many of the stories in his first volume came from his days as a park ranger/historian at Gettysburg, others came after the publication of his first book, from visitors to Gettysburg who just happened to run into one of the many spirits wafting about the great battlefield.

Some are things that happened to Nesbitt while he was living in historic houses on the park grounds. They have been validated by other rangers who lived in those houses before him.

Some stories came from older park rangers who patrolled the field in the 1950s and '60s. There was the story of sightings of a horseman, completely out of place, riding down the west slope of Little Round Top. His horse picked his steps very carefully around the brush and rocks; the rider could give him no direction through the reins because, the observers noticed just before the horseman and horse vanished, the rider was missing his head.

There are the other stories of the sightings of a "Woman in White," mostly in the vicinity of Spangler's Spring. She is seen "floating," by most descriptions, across the open fields around the stone structure housing the modern water fountain representing the original spring. Her actions have been described as moving, bending down, then moving on as if looking for something or someone in particular. Those exact motions had been repeated time and again shortly after the battle by nuns from a nearby convent acting as volunteer nurses, looking among the dead for those wounded soldiers that could still be helped. Once the Woman in White was seen actually materializing among the rocks and trees across from the spring, much to the horror and fascination of two nurses visiting the battlefield after dark. They testified to their encounter in a documentary that appeared on television.

But one of the earliest ghost stories about Gettysburg comes from the soldiers themselves.

The Union army's Fifth Corps had completed an arduous daylong march on July 1, 1863, from Maryland into Pennsylvania and was encamped for the night just west of Hanover, near McSherrystown. Exhausted, thirsty, hungry, they had just begun cooking their meager rations over their campfires in the dark when word spread through the camps: Douse the fires, pack up the half-cooked rations, wake up if you'd been lucky enough to eat quickly and then collapse into slumber. There had been a great clash of armies just a few miles to the west at a place called Gettysburg. An overnight forced march was ordered to reinforce their comrades in blue.

Weary, angry soldiers forced stiffened limbs to pack up gear and fall into marching columns. Slowly, like a massive, undulating animal, the men moved through the hot July darkness.

During a night march the view was less than spectacular: A soldier would see the knapsack of the soldier in front of him. Occasionally the twinkling of oil lamps being lit in the windows of curious farmers along the way would catch their attention. Mostly the rhythmic slogging along through the choking dust lulled the men into an almost dreamlike state.

Somewhere along the route a bizarre rumor began to be passed back through the column, met at first with derision and disbelief. The front ranks had seen a rider, apparently leading the route. He was, by his carriage, obviously a fine horseman. He would stop, allow the column to catch up, then ride ahead again, until he was barely out of sight. The times he could be seen most clearly, the men could make out as well that he was a military man, for he wore a uniform. There were troubling details, however.

His cape was longer than the modern military manual prescribed. And his hat was nothing like the "slouch" hats, or kepis, or "Hardee" hats officers wore. In fact, he wore military headgear completely out of date by some eighty years: a tricornered hat.

And, little by little as they continued to get brief glimpses of him—a profile here, a frontal view there—some thought they recognized him from the portraits hung in their one-room schoolhouses back home.

It was the ghost of none other than George Washington himself.

The identity of the spirit passed through the ranks like wind bending a prairie wheat field. Even the officers heard it. Years later, when he was asked about the specter who was leading the army, Major General Joshua L. Chamberlain, a lieutenant colonel in the Twentieth Maine at the time of the sightings, thought about it a long time before answering. According to historian John J. Pullen, the old general responded, "Yes, that report was circulated through our lines . . . Doubtless it was a superstition, but yet, who among us can say that such a thing was impossible?"

Most of the men were elated at what some had seen. They felt it was an omen: George Washington, the father of his country, stepping in from the spirit world to lead them to victory and save the Union he had founded.

Their enthusiasm might have been dampened had they stopped to remember two historical facts: first, that Washington was a Southerner—a Virginian by birth—and second, that he was considered, at least by the British, a rebel.

2

JOHN BROWN'S CURSE FROM THE GALLOWS

Drive a few miles outside of nearly any city in Pennsylvania and you will discover why the vast area was originally called "Penn's Woods." And with so much timber in the state, forest fires are a great concern. Everyone knows that just the smallest of sparks, with the forest in just the right degree of dryness, can cause an unstoppable inferno with a destructive life of its own.

This observation of Pennsylvania is an analogy for the whole of America for much of its history: a tinderbox of passions and emotions over an explosive condition that just would not go away. The subject had simmered near the flashpoint almost since the first settlers, through the colonial era, and certainly since the founding of the country and the Constitution.

The white-hot subject was human bondage. Slavery in the New World. And the small flicker that caught America on fire was nurtured—and saw its hottest conflagration—in Pennsylvania.

Slavery, of course, had been around since prebiblical times. It was a scourge on humanity that inflicted ill-treatment, suffering, and death to those unfortunate enough to become ensnared in it.

But to some of the founders of America, educated in the tenets of the Enlightenment, it was particularly odious because of the hypocrisy involved.

Philosophically, it didn't—couldn't—fit in the New World the founders of America envisioned, where "all men are created equal," endowed by their creator with certain unalienable rights: life, liberty, and the pursuit of happiness. How could these noble goals be reconciled with the forced, unpaid labor and ownership of other human beings?

If you think that we can't be talking about Pennsylvania—being north of the Mason-Dixon Line—then you're wrong. All of the colonies were guilty. Ships from God-fearing New England sailed to the west coast of Africa, where they picked up blacks who just days before had been farming and hunting and living peacefully in their villages with their families and friends, admiring their neighbors' newly made clothing as they prepared their homes and children for dinner. They suddenly were set upon by black "slavers" who tore them away from their homes, stripped them, chained them, and marched them to the coast.

There, they and their neighbors stood naked before strangers who bid upon them. Strong-backed husbands were taken from wives and children; the leaders of the communities were thrown in with the lot and all were driven, like cattle, into the dank, miserable, black holds of the slave ships to endure—or perish in—the Middle Passage. For the weeks-long trip across the Atlantic, they saw the outside of the ship's hold perhaps once a day. The rest of the time they lay in the human waste and vomit and bilge that collected in the hold. Those that died were thrown overboard.

To the slavers—white and black—they were cargo, a commodity that would pay well once they reached the New World, where labor was needed.

As they arrived in ports in the colonies—Philadelphia being one of them—they were brought from the hold, the smell of crowded, unwashed humanity wafting through the air. Their ears were bombarded with an unknown gibberish. Chained, they were placed upon a stage or a block of stone, still naked, to be poked and prodded and bid upon. For many, there would be one last glimpse of a husband or wife and children. The auctioneer's gavel would descend, and they would be carted off along with strangers to a far-off workplace in Pennsylvania, New York, New England, Maryland, Virginia, or farther south.

Africans were not the only slaves in America at the time. The Irish, too, became victims of this hideous system. But somewhere along the line, "indentured" white slaves were eventually freed; black slaves continued to be held in bondage.

And whites were not the only slaveholders. The first legally recognized slaveholder in the colonies was an African American man. One of the largest slaveholders in Louisiana was an African American woman who utilized 152 slaves to run her large sugar plantation. A large number of free African-Americans held slaves in Charleston, South Carolina.

No less human than the whites, slaves were not treated as such when it came to human rights. "Society" took over; "just the way things are" took over; eventually even the US government took over with laws sanctioning slavery, determining that, for census purposes, a slave counted as three-fifths of a person. Because slavery was prosperous in one section of the country and not in another, the nation divided. As new territories were added, Congress negotiated whether the territory should enter the Union as "free" or "slave," as much for the political power balance as the morality of it. Eventually slaveholders in some of the states released their slaves, but only when they didn't need them to produce income anymore, when another economic system made it prudent. The federal Fugitive Slave Act made it illegal to even assist a slave to escape.

Eventually the country began to grow a conscience about the "peculiar institution" that made some men lord over others.

But it appeared that weighing conscience against profits is never a fair balance.

Soon groups decided to abolish slavery, led by fiery ministers and politicians bent upon maintaining their power base. Pennsylvania was the first state to abolish slavery, perhaps because of the Quaker influence in the state. Others followed suit, mostly north of the famed "Mason and Dixon's Line." They were responding to the burgeoning

Industrial Revolution and mechanized industry, less dependent upon a large labor force. But many northern industries needed raw materials, especially cotton from the southern states, the cultivating of which was labor intensive, requiring the continuation of the odious system of slavery.

Periodically there were attempts by the slaves themselves to cast off their chains. New York had one of the largest slave populations in the colonies, and in 1712 a group of twenty-three slaves rebelled in New York City by setting a fire, then attacking the men who responded. Using guns, hatchets, and swords, they killed nine whites. Some seventy slaves were rounded up and twenty-one eventually executed by burning to death. Fear of another slave insurrection provoked government officials to use the most severe form of execution available and then enact draconian laws disallowing blacks to carry firearms, gather in groups of more than three, or gamble. Theft, rape, conspiracy, and property damage by slaves became punishable by death.

The Stono Rebellion in 1739 saw slaves battle militia as they attempted to make their way from South Carolina to Florida. Some eighty slave "soldiers" burned seven plantations and killed twenty-five whites on their march until they fought a pitched battle with white militiamen on September 11, killing twenty militiamen and losing forty-four rebels. Within a week another battle was fought that ended their march to Florida with executions and deportations.

A series of fires in New York City in 1741 was attributed to slaves attempting rebellion, but the proceedings became more like the Salem witch trials, with neighbor accusing neighbor, resulting in burning the allegedly guilty at the stake.

Gabriel's Rebellion in 1800 centered around the Virginia capital of Richmond, which Gabriel intended to invade. He was betrayed by fellow slaves and he, his two brothers, and twenty-three others involved in the insurrection were hanged.

On Dunbar Creek, on Saint Simon's Island near Savannah, Georgia, a cargo of Igbo tribespeople from Nigeria, known for their fierce resistance to chattel slavery, took over the slave ship on which they were being transported. After drowning the crew they grounded the ship. Having already spent some of their lives in slavery and knowing what lay ahead, they marched into the creek, committing suicide. Their act today is revered by many as the ultimate rebellion to slavery. As if to accentuate the deed, the site of Ebo Landing is said to be haunted by the spirits of the rebellious slaves who died rather than submit.

Denmark Vesey, a carpenter and minister who had purchased his own freedom, organized a slave rebellion in 1820 in Charleston, South Carolina, by attempting to raise a slave army. The plan was apparently quite elaborate, with a multipronged attack on the Charleston Arsenal to capture arms, the killing of slaveholders to free other slaves, and the commandeering of ships in Charleston Harbor to sail to Haiti, site of a successful slave rebellion years before. Word of the rebellion necessarily got out to the many slaves in Charleston. Some slaves loyal to their masters told them of the plot, and a dragnet began. Though no arms caches were ever found and actual organization of the rebellion was sketchy, Vesey and five others were captured, tried, and eventually hanged on July 2, 1822.

In 1831, in Southampton County, Virginia, slave rebellion drew blood again.

Nat Turner was a precocious slave child who, despite laws prohibiting it, learned to read and write. As he grew into manhood he found religion and became respected among his fellow slaves for his intelligence and fervor. Fasting, praying, and immersing himself in the Bible led to visions, and his preaching led other slaves to name him "the Prophet." The visions grew more intense and ominous until, on February 11, 1831, he witnessed a total eclipse of the sun, which he took as the final sign to plan his rebellion to free his fellow slaves. Another solar event on August 13—when the sun turned bluish green—convinced him that the time was ripe. After dark on August 21, Turner and his band began invading the homes of their masters, killing whole families using axes, hatchets, swords, and knives so as not to alert their neighbors with gunshots. From farm to farm they went, murdering slave owners and their families—including children—as they slept, and gathering (sometimes reluctantly) the newly freed slaves as part of their seventy-man "army." Militias were called out, and within two days the rebellion was quashed. Blacks with even a suspicion of being involved were murdered, but Turner temporarily hid in a hole in a local farmer's field. In the terrible backlash some two hundred blacks were killed and Turner and fifty-six of his followers were executed.

You would think that slave owners would soon realize how antiquated, immoral, and impractical the system of slavery was.

Indeed, after so many slave insurrections, each generation of slaveholders grew more suspicious and more paranoid and their reactions to quell the rebellion more harsh.

And abolitionists grew more zealous in their cause, pointing out at every step that slaveholders were living in sin by holding their fellow humans in bondage. To the slaveholder, after generations in the system, it had become a social institution, somewhat like marriage. Once slavery became institutionalized, condemnation would be like someone telling a married couple that, for the last thirty or forty years, they had been living in sin. Of course the accuser would have been scoffed at as a lunatic or worse.

Then there were the political factors, which may be too numerous to elaborate upon in this work. Suffice it to say that as the election of 1860 approached, the country was firmly divided between slave and free states, and whoever was elected president would probably tip the scales one way or the other.

It was a nation of dry, combustible tinder waiting to explode. Into this fuel, heated to the flashpoint, stepped John Brown.

Born in 1800, in Connecticut, Brown moved to Oberlin, Ohio, with his family when he was five. Oberlin was the site of Oberlin Institute (now Oberlin College), a center of liberal thought. He left home at sixteen to attend school in Massachusetts, then Connecticut, but returned to Ohio and married in 1820. He learned the tannery business and became a Pennsylvanian. By 1825 Brown had started his own tannery in New Richmond, Pennsylvania. His businesses expanded into raising cattle and surveying, but a series of personal setbacks left him in dire straits. In 1831 one of his sons died, he himself fell ill, and his wife died shortly after childbirth. By 1833, however, he had remarried and moved to Kent, Ohio. By 1842 Brown was declared officially bankrupt. But sometime before that, no doubt from coming to age in the era of slaveholder versus abolitionist, his passions had been fired by the cruelty and injustice of the slavery system in America.

In 1837 abolitionist publisher Elijah P. Lovejoy of slaveholding St. Louis moved to free-state Alton, Illinois, but had his fourth printing press destroyed and was savagely murdered by pro-slavery men. The attack on freedom of the press and the invasion into a free state to assassinate a publisher moved Brown greatly, and he swore an oath, from that day forth, to dedicate his life to the destruction of slavery in the United States.

Back in Ohio he started a sheep and wool business, then moved to Springfield, Massachusetts, and was, through his travels, brought into contact with fervent abolitionists. He began to attend a black church while in Springfield and heard speakers like Frederick Douglass and Sojourner Truth. He grew more and more dedicated to slavery eradication. In Springfield he was exposed to the highly secretive Underground Railroad, a vast network of clandestine people and places set up to help slaves escape from the American South. He also organized a militant group for those ends. The Fugitive Slave Act was passed during this time and continued to galvanize Brown's antislavery sentiment.

In 1855, hearing that pro-slavery men were violently attempting to intimidate free-staters, Brown went to Kansas. On the night of May 24, 1856, he and his band kidnapped five pro-slavery men and hacked them to death with swords. Brown had ushered in a period that the press dubbed "Bleeding Kansas."

"Battles" between pro-slavery groups and free-staters raged through the state. Brown's homestead was destroyed and Brown's son Frederick was killed.

By November 1856 Brown was raising money for his cause among New England abolitionists. They pledged to supply Brown with two hundred new Sharps breech-loading rifles—state of the art for the time—but wanted to remain anonymous. Brown also ordered one thousand pikes, an ancient weapon he felt slaves could easily handle with little training. He hired a British mercenary to drill and train his men and write tactical guidelines. Clearly he was planning some violent military action.

He continued to travel and raise money and support as his plans jelled. He wrote a provisional constitution to govern the freed slaves where his army invaded. He named himself commander-in-chief of his army and appointed a secretary of war, a secretary of state, and a president for his provisional government and wrote a Declaration of Liberty for the slaves in the territory he planned to invade. He met with Harriet Tubman, the courageous runaway slave who had returned numerous times to the slaveholding states to lead groups of other escaped slaves northward. From her he gathered information on the network of safe houses in Pennsylvania and other border states.

Beginning in June 1859 Brown rented the upstairs room of a house on East King Street (now #225) in Chambersburg, Pennsylvania, under the alias of Isaac Smith, an iron mine developer. Known as the Ritner Boarding House, it was run by the daughter-in-law of former Pennsylvania governor Joseph Ritner, a major personality in the Pennsylvania abolitionist movement. It was in this house that Brown began to gather tools and receive weapons and information for his raid into the South.

Mr. "Smith" evidently fit in well in the community, according to one source, teaching Sunday school classes, preaching a sermon at a local church, selling charcoal to Chambersburg commercial furnaces, and even opening a sawmill. It was all a cover for his true mission of planning a military assault upon the institution of slavery in the United States.

On July 3 he visited, for reconnaissance purposes, Harpers Ferry, Virginia (now West Virginia), site of a US arsenal filled with armaments. While in the area he rented a farmhouse in Maryland some eighteen miles from Harpers Ferry to be the final jumping-off point for his invasion to free the slaves.

Returning to the house on King Street in Chambersburg, Brown began to finalize his plans. Several of his conspirators, including three of his sons, had now moved to Chambersburg. He asked Harriet Tubman to recruit from escaped slaves living in Canada for his army. As always, totally devoted to the cause, she did. He met for two days with Frederick Douglass at the Chambersburg house in August and revealed his plan, which was to begin with a raid upon the US Armory at Harpers Ferry to capture arms. There he asked Douglass to join his army.

Douglass turned him down and tried to dissuade him from pursuing his plans. But by the time Brown was in Chambersburg, he was committed to military action. (Douglass had learned of Brown's plan earlier and had been actively dissuading blacks from joining him. He was convinced that Brown's plan held no hope of success and would only make slaveholders tighten their bonds upon their slaves.)

In September the pikes arrived. More crates came by train addressed to "Smith & Sons," allegedly mining tools and equipment for Smith's company. In reality they were the Sharps rifles and ammunition, to be transported to the Kennedy farmhouse in Maryland. Military plans were developed for a force of 4,500 men to march into the slaveholding states, seizing the arms at Harpers Ferry first. As they progressed southward, Brown expected newly freed slaves in the zones of liberation to flock to his side and enlist in his army. They would fight self-defensive battles only, depleting first Virginia, then all the other slaveholding states of their economic lifeblood, causing collapse of their sinful system.

The plans laid in Chambersburg were grandiose, to say the least. Instead of 4,500 men, Brown could gather only 21. On October 16, 1859, eighteen of those left the Kennedy farmhouse on their way to Harpers Ferry.

The night raid was a surprise on the sleepy town at the confluence of the Potomac and Shenandoah Rivers. The armory was easily captured and telegraph wires were cut, isolating the town. Raiders were sent out and civilian hostages, including the great-grand-nephew of George Washington, were taken. The raiders spread the word to the slaves that their hour of liberation was upon them; all they needed to do was come to Harpers Ferry and join John Brown.

The initial stages went well. But then a B & O train approached Harpers Ferry from the west and was stopped by Brown's guards. When the baggage handler tried to warn the passengers, he was shot and killed by Brown's men. Hayward Shepherd, a free African American employed by the railroad, became the first casualty in Brown's war on slavery. For some reason Brown's men allowed the train to continue to Baltimore. Along the way train personnel alerted the authorities that armed insurrection was going on in Harpers Ferry. The insurrectionists were identified as abolitionists.

The townspeople had already begun to react to the invasion and taking of hostages. Instead of thousands of slaves swarming to Brown's side, armed civilians from surrounding farms occupied strategic positions around Harpers Ferry and began taking potshots at Brown's men. Brown consolidated his force in the fire engine house within the armory yard and returned fire. Casualties began to mount on each side.

Militia units arrived at the town the next day and sealed off Brown's escape route. Firing continued throughout the day. Brown sent his son Watson and another raider out under a flag of truce, but townspeople refused to honor it and shot the pair. Oliver, another son, was shot inside the engine house.

Overnight, a contingent of US Marines arrived and surrounded the engine house. They were commanded by an army engineer, Colonel Robert E. Lee, later to become one of the most famous generals in American history. His volunteer aide also bore a name that was soon to become famous: J. E. B. Stuart.

Stuart approached the engine house with Lee's demand for surrender. Brown wanted to parley, but Stuart's orders precluded honoring any demands from insurrectionists who had just assaulted a US armory. He waved his hat and the marines attacked.

The fight was over quickly, and Brown and his men were captured. In their "war" on slavery, they had killed four and wounded nine others.

Brown lost ten, including two sons. One of his sons escaped along with four other fighters, and seven men were captured with Brown.

Brown's trial began as soon as he had recovered sufficiently from wounds suffered in the engine house fight. He was still confined to a cot during the proceedings. It seemed that Brown was resigned to his fate and even embraced the fact that he was to become a martyr. While he could perhaps foresee his own death by hanging on December 2, 1859, what he could not foresee was the conflagration of biblical proportions that would ensue from the spark he carried into Harpers Ferry.

On the morning of his execution he prophesized, in writing, "I, John Brown, am now quite certain that the crimes of this guilty land will never be purged away but with blood. I had, as I now think, vainly flattered myself that without very much bloodshed it might be done."

But even John Brown could not prophesy the amount of blood that would be needed to purge away the guilt of the curse of slavery.

Brown's name became a watchword around the country. To abolitionists it was a rallying cry: "As He died to make men holy, let us die to make men free" sang soldiers fighting for the Federal army, using the tune from "John Brown's Body," a well-known marching song for Union troops.

To Southerners his name represented the specter of slave insurrection, of trusted servants taking up household implements and killing their masters in the dead of night. Later, as they raised their own armies and captured government installations in the South, Brown's actions would be seen as the catalyst that allowed armed Federals to invade their southern homeland.

In four years the American Civil War bled the nation of an entire generation of young men. For years the figure quoted was 620,000 men dead at the end of the war. More recent figures, based on census records rather than army figures, which were often fudged for public relations purposes, have brought the grand total of corpses to as high as 850,000.

Today, given that the US population has grown tenfold, that would be like losing more than eight million human beings in just four years of contemporary warfare.

And Pennsylvania was inextricably woven into the matrix of America's bloodiest war.

John Brown's Tannery in New Richmond, Pennsylvania, close to Meadville, is on the National Register of Historic Places. It is one of several places in the country that are preserved as testaments to his life. The tannery building is in ruins now, but apparently something of Brown, not quite of this world, remains.

Periodically, a tall figure is seen moving among the ruins as if still laboring at the long-gone tannery. A black man is also seen in spirit form, perhaps looking for the man who will help him to freedom, martyred over a century and a half ago. If the paranormal theory that intense human passions draw and retain spirits to a place is true, then John Brown's Tannery would be a prime candidate.

The Ritner Boarding House also has its whispers of ghostly pacings, noises, voices, and sightings.

But even more associated with the man who helped bring freedom to the enslaved and death by the hundreds of thousands to the nation is a site in Pennsylvania that far surpasses any in America for its concentrated bloodshed in the fratricidal war that doomed slavery. Though he died three and a half years before, Brown's efforts led to the one watershed battle that broke the military back of the slaveholding states, and whose name remains seared on the American consciousness, a blessing for the Union, a curse for the Confederates: Gettysburg.

3

IVERSON'S PITS

"Deep and long must the desolate homes and orphan children of North Carolina rue the rashness of that hour."

So wrote a captain in the Twenty-Third North Carolina Regiment who fought at the Battle of Gettysburg. The hour he's writing about is three o'clock on the afternoon of July 1, 1863. He was a member of Brigadier General Alfred Iverson's Brigade of North Carolinians. In the final official records of another regiment of the brigade are written the words, "Initiated at Seven Pines, sacrificed at Gettysburg, surrendered at Appomattox."

What could have happened on those sun-splashed fields to the northwest of the small town of Gettysburg in just a few short minutes that could have made such an impression on those Southerners who fought there and those at home who were left behind? What horror could have left such an impression on even the land that, since shortly after the battle, the area named "Iverson's Pits" has maintained the dubious distinction of being haunted by those who were sacrificed?

When it happened, the battle that would become known as the most massive in the Civil War and costliest in terms of lives had been raging for several hours. The fighting that began on the road to Cashtown between Confederate infantry and Union cavalry had snowballed and stretched into the fields farther north and east as more Southern and Northern units arrived to concentrate on the town that had eleven roads all radiating from within a block of its center square. As part of the massive Confederate invasion of the state, some of the units had been in Carlisle, Pennsylvania, only thirty miles north of Gettysburg. Carlisle was the site of a US Army barracks, where many

Confederate officers had been stationed before the war as leaders of the "Old Army."

It was a strange homecoming. Some of the officers looked up old friends from the town, now officially their enemies. Others found quantities of liquor and lager beer and partook to extremes, at least in part for old time's sake. Then they got the orders to march on Gettysburg and woozily began the journey.

As Iverson's men marched southward toward Gettysburg, they had no idea what they were in for. Once in position, they knew that the two brigades that were to protect their flanks had already been repulsed. What they did not know was that one of the brigades on the left had pushed the Union flank back so that it had doubled back upon itself. The Union survivors had taken refuge, crouching behind one of the ubiquitous stone walls, and placed their flags upon the ground so that they were virtually hidden from sight.

Thirty-four-year-old Alfred Iverson had a distinguished military career before the Battle of Gettysburg. He was the son of a US senator from Georgia and dropped out of military school at age seventeen to join his father's regiment in the Mexican War. Though he tried his hand at running a railroad and studying law, he had a natural affinity for the military, and through his father's political influence, he gained an officer's commission in the newly formed First US Cavalry Regiment. He fought the "Border Ruffians" in Kansas and Nebraska, and against the Indians, then rode on the Mormon Expedition. At the outbreak of the Civil War he helped organize the Twentieth North Carolina Regiment, was wounded during the Seven Days Battles in defense of Richmond, and rejoined his unit to fight at Antietam—called the Battle of Sharpsburg in the South—on September 17, 1862. But it was his experience at Chancellorsville, less than two months before Gettysburg, that may have quenched his thirst for combat. There he was struck in the groin by a spent bullet, causing a "contusion" that made even walking painful.

So, it may be understandable why, in the very next battle, he ended up commanding from the rear the brigade that bore his name.

He ordered his troops into the battle, then retired to the safety of a solid chestnut log from which he repeatedly reminded his staff that looking over the log needlessly exposed one. Without reconnoitering the ground over which his men were to attack, or sending out skirmishers ahead of them to draw out the enemy, his orders to them were meaningless: "Give them hell!"

His men began their march from Oak Hill, near where the Eternal Light Peace Memorial now stands on the battlefield. They crossed the Mummasburg Road and into the fields of farmer John Forney. As one survivor put it, "The enemy's position was not known to the troops. The alignment of the brigade was a false alignment and the men were left to die without help or guidance."

During the Civil War, protocol demanded that officers lead their men into battle, so Iverson remaining in the rear behind cover was conspicuous.

The brigade wandered in its battle line across the undulating fields, seemingly lost and searching for an enemy to fight. The fields in their front were so devoid of activity that no doubt some of the veterans of so many battles got suspicious. Within seconds their fears were confirmed.

The left flank got to within eighty yards of the stone wall on the edge of the ridge that led into Gettysburg. Suddenly, from that wall rose several lines of infantry in blue leveling their muskets. Officers in Iverson's Brigade barely had time to issue orders to halt, let alone aim and fire, when the Union troops loosed a devastating volley that sent hundreds of well-aimed minié balls crashing into the closely packed North Carolinians. Many did not survive that first volley, as evidence would show after the battle; many more were wounded. A Union soldier witnessed that "hundreds of Confederates fell under that first volley."

As for those who survived the devastating first fusillade, the only thing they could do was lie down in a natural ditch that crossed the field. The Union fire continued. Any Confederate who raised himself up to fire was doomed. Some of the men attempted to surrender, waving white rags. Iverson saw this and thought his brigade was surrendering. Later, apparently forgetting his own conduct during the battle, he wrote that he thought this act "disgraceful."

The show of white prompted a Union regiment to rush into the field and bring back 213 officers and men of Iverson's Brigade as prisoners.

Iverson's men were pinned down until the Union line, with increased Confederate pressure from the west and north, and new pressure from Confederates attacking from the northeast, began to implode. The two wings of the Union army began a retreat back through the streets of Gettysburg, followed hotly by Confederates. The men of Iverson's Brigade who were not captured were temporarily left behind where they fought and where many of their comrades died.

Of the 1,470 men who crossed the Mummasburg Road and marched into farmer Forney's fields, 512 were killed or wounded and 308 were missing, presumably captured. Iverson himself wrote that after the battle, when he finally went out to be with his men, he found 500 of them lying dead or wounded in a line as straight as if they had been "on dress parade." One officer from the North Carolina Twenty-Third said it was the only time in the entire war he saw blood flow "in a rivulet," there at the bottom of the ditch where Iverson's men took cover.

When the burial parties finally got to that part of the field to do their hideous work, one private of the North Carolina regiment was found dead, his hands still gripping his musket, with five bullets driven into his head.

A Confederate artilleryman, apparently after some of the bodies had already been buried or removed, saw "79 North Carolinians laying dead in a straight line . . . perfectly dressed. Three had fallen to the front, the rest had fallen backward, yet the feet of all these dead men were in a perfectly straight line. . . . They had all evidently been killed by one volley of musketry and they had fallen in their tracks without a single struggle."

Most people do not realize that the soldiers who died at Gettysburg were buried at least twice. First they were buried where they fell, sometimes by their comrades if they had time before moving on, often by burial parties after the battle, occasionally by the farmers upon whose land they were slain. The burials were hasty and the graves were shallow, usually with no presiding clergy to consecrate the site. When the rains came and the bodies swelled, Gettysburg-area housewives were treated to the sight out their kitchen windows of a grizzled hand or leg or head popping out of their gardens-turned-cemeteries. It was too much.

Husbands got the word in no uncertain terms. They, in turn, contacted their government representatives in Harrisburg. Governor Curtin, Pennsylvania's wartime leader, gathered funds and told local Gettysburg attorney David Wills to do something about the problem. Wills bought seventeen acres on Cemetery Hill, site of the civilian Evergreen Cemetery, and exhumations and reburials began in earnest.

On November 19, 1863, Abraham Lincoln and his entourage dedicated and consecrated the new "National Cemetery." And so the Union dead lay in consecrated ground. But only the Union dead.

The Confederates, deemed unworthy of burial next to those patriots they may have had a hand in killing, were left on the battlefield, in those shallow graves, to be cared for (or not cared for) by the kindness of the strangers upon whose land they happened to die.

Therefore, Iverson's men, first sacrificed by military blunder, suffered the ignominy of lying in a long ditch, their uniforms and blankets as their winding sheets, unembalmed, in the hated, unconsecrated Yankee soil until finally, in 1870–71, Southern women contracted a Gettysburg man to exhume the bodies—or what was left of them—and ship them south to their own "National Cemeteries."

Cleft in farmer Forney's fields was one depression (and perhaps two), very long and about the height of a man.

In the years after the war, surviving veterans returned to Gettysburg to see the fields where they had once struggled and lost so many comrades. The North Carolinians of Iverson's Brigade were astounded to see the outline of the burial site of their fellow soldiers, with grass growing so much greener there than in the surrounding fields that they could trace it with their walking sticks. A captain from the North Carolina Twenty-Third dug into the bright green depression and found "a veritable mine of war relics," no doubt released into the earth as the men completed their transformation "from dust to dust."

They, no doubt, also heard the rumors, perhaps from farmer Forney himself, that as dusk began to draw its veil across what came to be known locally as "Iverson's Pits," his workers would come scurrying back to the farmhouse and refuse to work that area. It was what they heard that terrified them.

From out of nowhere they heard orders being shouted. And taps from invisible drums. They strained to hear echoes of bugle calls carrying across the fields, and the awful but unmistakable sounds of lead bullets hitting flesh, over and over and over.

Farmer Forney tried ridiculing them, then shaming them, but they would not budge, because the worst were the unearthly screams they heard that seemed to emanate from the pits themselves.

And into the present, tales of what seems impossible still emerge from the area. There have been several sightings of a horseman—a courier, no doubt, because of his urgency—who rides at breakneck speed southward down Oak Ridge and stops in the vicinity of what is now the Doubleday Inn, a modern bed-and-breakfast. Witnesses have seen him dismount, but when they reach the inn, there is no rider and no horse tied up outside. It is then they realize they have been victimized by the Other World.

A family walking the area on a winter's night heard voices coming from the woods. At first they thought it was a party, but they soon dismissed the notion as they entered the woods and walked toward the noise. As they got closer the sounds grew fainter until, when the family felt they had reached the source, the sounds died completely.

Other stories have emerged from the area, enough to elicit two chapters in Mark Nesbitt's series *Ghosts of Gettysburg*. But none boggles the mind as much as one fifteen-second tape recording made one night several years ago by a member of author Patty Wilson's ghost research group. They had been investigating the Iverson's Pits area and it was approaching ten o'clock at night, the time the national park closes. Patty mentioned to everyone that they had to wrap up their investigation and return to town. One woman, who was recording the investigation, felt compelled to say one last thing to the spirits of Iverson's Brigade, sacrificed upon that ground, then virtually forgotten as they lay buried in Yankee territory. "God be with you," she is heard to say on the tape, giving her own benediction to those forlorn souls. A second or two passes, then, echoing from the past, unheard by her but recorded on the tape, is a drawn-out human scream of agony, unexplainable by any modern means available, but existing in this world nonetheless.

4

GETTYSBURG—
CURSED TO BE A
KILLING FIELD?

The Battle of Gettysburg, fought in south-central Pennsylvania July 1–3, 1863, stands out as one of the most singular events of violence in all of American history.

But was it all that singular?

On June 30, 1863, the day before the great battle, the soldiers passing over their future combat zone saw the scene as common rolling farm fields checkered with field-stone fences, broken here and there by squat hills and occasional woodlots. There was nothing to distinguish it from any other mid-nineteenth-century rural American place they knew.

In the next three days, they themselves would transform the peaceful setting into a charnel house: blood-smeared, littered with human bodies and parts of bodies, and those wounded and alive writhing in a horrible nightmare scene.

Fifty-one thousand crimson-stained human beings remained in the fields and town after the armies marched away on July 4 and 5. Included in that casualty figure were the dead, bloating in the summer sun, then soaked by the torrential rains that followed the battle; the wounded, taken to makeshift shelters or structures in town to be operated upon; and the missing: the living who ran away, or those who were simply liquidated by cannon shot, blown to pieces, now unrecognizable as individual human beings.

When the two armies were finished, the Federals had won and the Confederates retreated, never to invade that far north again. The battle has been called "the High Tide of the Confederacy," the closest Confederates came to victory in the four years of the American Civil War.

The strange part is, in spite of the importance of the battle, it may not have been the first to be fought on this very same piece of earth. Could it be that what we now call Gettysburg was cursed to become a battlefield forever?

Not that fighting two major battles on the same battleground is all that unusual. Throughout history, battles have often been fought over the same piece of ground. Europe is replete with fields that were fought over more than once over the centuries: the Marne, Ypres, Artois in the First World War, for example. Krithia became a battlefield three times in that war.

Our own Civil War saw two battles fought at Manassas, two through the streets of Fredericksburg, and numerous battles around Winchester, Virginia, which changed hands more than seventy times during the war.

But these instances occurred because there was some strategic importance to the site: Manassas was a railroad junction; Fredericksburg was situated directly between Washington and Richmond, the two capitals of the warring sections; and Winchester was on the main road in the Shenandoah Valley, the much fought-over breadbasket of the Confederacy.

But neither commander wanted to fight in Gettysburg. There was no major railroad junction—in fact, the railroad stopped a block north of the center of town, unfinished to the west. Major General George G. Meade, the commander of the Union army, was ordered to keep his troops between the invading Confederates and Washington, the capital of the North. General Robert E. Lee would have liked to have fought farther north or east, perhaps capturing Harrisburg, the capital of Pennsylvania, or Philadelphia, the major port of Pennsylvania and the city where the United States was born.

So, instead of being a strategic destination, like so many other battlefields, Gettysburg, destined to become the largest, costliest battle ever on the North American continent, was where the two massive armies brushed against one another, entangled, and wouldn't let go until they both nearly bled to death.

The site of the largest battle ever fought on the North American continent may actually be the site of *two* of the largest battles ever fought on the continent. Rumors of a huge battle between Native American tribes on what would later become the Civil War battlefield of Gettysburg have floated from the earliest settlers.

Reports from hunters who heard Native American war whoops were whispered to wives long after the children had gone to bed or to sometimes skittish, disbelieving friends after a little of the applejack was consumed. "Out by the Devil's Den was where I heard 'em, clear as could be. Sun was about to set when I heard 'em. Got out real quick."

One of the earliest stories Mark Nesbitt recorded in his series predates the Civil War–era battle. Two hunters had lost track of time and near dusk found themselves lost in the tangled boulders of the ridge known as Devil's Den. It was growing cold, and they were fearful of having to camp unprepared with the late fall weather about to close in on them. From the lengthening shadows in the distance, they saw a figure, dressed rather strangely, signaling for them to follow. With nothing to lose, they tried to catch up with him but failed to get anything but glimpses of him in the labyrinth of rock. The glimpses they got, however, indicated someone from an earlier era: long, dark braided hair, buckskin shirt, moccasins—clearly the image of a man whose race had been chased from this land hundreds of years before.

He led them to an area they were familiar with. They turned to thank him, but he was gone, vanished, it seemed, back into the granite maze, back into the time period from which he came.

Mark also recalls that, as a young national park ranger in Gettysburg, he would be invited to friends' homes and the conversation would turn to artifacts of the battle. After being assured that all the artifacts were picked up on private land, he was shown a mason jar filled to the brim with minié balls, the common bullet used by both Union and Confederate soldiers during the 1863 battle. On at least two occasions he remembers being shown another mason jar, filled to the top with arrowheads, also collected near the national park. "There had to be more arrowheads than bullets since they took up less space in the jar," he says. "To me this was evidence of at least as many arrows having been fired as bullets, which could possibly mean at least as many armed Indians battling as Civil War soldiers."

Though no Native America burial sites have been located within the park boundaries and none has been found—or at least not made public—in the vicinity, it is well known that unpreserved bodies and bones leave little trace of themselves after several centuries due to animal and insect predation.

One source says the Indian tribal war happened two hundred years before the battle of Gettysburg. Another says the site is even older and may predate the discovery of America by Columbus.

There is local documentation for the apparently huge battle that took place somewhere near the Gettysburg hills the white man would name Big Round Top and Little Round Top.

In 1880 a Gettysburg man, Emmanuel Bushman, published an article that mentioned "many unnatural and supernatural sights and sounds" coming from the region of Big and Little Round Top. He called this area the "Indian Fields." Early settlers to the area had told tales of ghosts roaming the woods and among the rocks and of hearing what they called "war whoops" echoing through the trees at night. This was, of course, years after the last Native Americans had vacated the land.

Bushman wrote again, in 1884, about a tribe having lived near what is now called Devil's Den. He thought the boulders may have been part of a great pyramid that had been destroyed by some catastrophic blast that left its mark on the rocks.

How much of this tale was a figment of Bushman's imagination, or local folklore that he recorded, can only be speculated. That Native

Americans used pyramids—like the ancient Egyptians—is undeniable; the evidence is abundant in South America. It also remains a mystery to some just how primitive cultures built structures that, under scientific scrutiny, appear to have needed modern technology to construct, moving massive stones too heavy to be moved without at least the wheel, or fitting stones together with the preciseness of steel or diamond cuts in an age before those technologies were available.

Numerous tribes settled in or traveled through the area of south-central Pennsylvania, including the Shawnee, Lenape, and Susquehannocks. A small map on the Internet has the line between the Susquehannocks and Shawnee from the Ohio Valley maddeningly close to where Gettysburg is now located. Could there have been a violent territorial dispute between the two long before the white man settled there?

Even more intriguing is that a name was given to the battle that allegedly took place at Indian Fields: the Battle of the Crows.

Talk to nearly anyone who has visited Gettysburg and they will likely mention that it indeed is a special place, infusing the visitor with emotions that are unexplainable. As one visitor said, coming to Gettysburg is like going into a church: You know it is just a building, but there is a special feeling about it. Could those special feelings be the psychic remnant that abides from some unknown supernatural force left in the now calm, bucolic fields around the town of Gettysburg? Could Gettysburg have been doomed to repeat as a killing ground?

5

VENGEANCE AT DEVIL'S DEN

One of the most famous photographs taken during the American Civil War is of a dead Confederate soldier lying behind a stone barricade, rifle leaning against one of the huge boulders in Devil's Den at Gettysburg.

Taken by the team of Alexander Gardner and Timothy O'Sullivan on July 6, 1863, it is one of the more poignant photographs in all of wartime photography. The sheer starkness of the black-and-white picture, the youth of the soldier, and the abject loneliness of his death capture the universal heartbreak of war. The only problem is that it was posed.

For years Devil's Den has been known as a place where cameras often malfunction. From cheap, throwaway cameras to expensive 35 millimeters, to digital still and video cameras, to professional TV cameras, all types have exhibited dead batteries, jams, strange exposures, and other glitches.

It has happened numerous times to author Mark Nesbitt, mostly in what is known as the "Triangular Field" adjacent to Devil's Den.

The first time it happened he was doing a photographic "sweep" of the Triangular Field, from the bottom, up the hill toward Devil's Den. "I was with two other photographers, both artists, who needed all the shots they could get," he says. On the way to Devil's Den he told them about the rumors that he had heard while working as a park ranger, stories about cameras failing in the area. Halfway up the slope is where he began having unexplainable trouble with his camera. "It was the most sophisticated, expensive 35 millimeter camera I'd ever owned. It had never failed me in the past. Suddenly it jammed.

"I stopped in the field and was trying to work the lever, thinking, 'Here I am on a contract and my equipment fails me.' Then I looked a few yards away to my client and realized his camera had jammed, too. Looking past him to the other artist, his son, I saw that he was playing with his broken camera," Mark recalls.

They all looked at each other. The older artist said jokingly, "Well, I guess the ghosts don't want us here!" They continued up to the parking lot and the car. As they were driving out of the Devil's Den area, the son, who was in the backseat fiddling with his camera, said, "Hey, my camera's working again." The father handed his camera back to the son. Before long there was the familiar "click, click, click" as his camera began to work again. "By the time we got back to town," Mark says, "my camera was working again as well."

A local television crew was doing a Halloween special and contacted Mark. He told them about the Devil's Den/Triangular Field's curse on cameras, and they decided to film Mark telling his the story there.

"I was standing in the Triangular Field at the top near the road through Devil's Den, reviewing what I was going to say with the producer," Mark remembers. "Over his shoulder I saw the cameraman scratching his head with the back of the camera open. Then he called to the producer to come over."

Mark watched while the two men poked and prodded the buttons inside the camera. A few minutes later the producer came back. "I have no idea what's going on up there, but all the LED lights are either yellow or red. They've always been green, for the eight years I've been working with that camera. It's self-adjusting. I can't figure it out."

Mark couldn't help but smile.

Several years later another crew from a different television station came to Gettysburg and wanted to re-create the event and film it; producers called the original camera crew and director in to explain what had happened. The original crew was set up in their positions when the new crew came in and began to set up. Mark remembers that "the cameraman brought in three battery belts and laid them on the ground in the Triangular Field. I was thinking, 'That may not be such a good idea.'"

Sure enough, as they were getting ready to film the re-creation, the cameraman said, "Wait. Something's wrong. This battery belt is dead."

He took it off, picked up another from the ground, put it on, and plugged it in. Looking through the camera, he uttered an oath and said, "This one's dead, too."

As he picked up the third battery belt he commented that he didn't understand it: He had charged the belts in the van all the way from the studio in Lancaster, over an hour away. They all should have been fully charged. He plugged in the third belt and said, "I only have a trickle on this one. Let's hurry up!"

The interviewer had to apologize to the audience before the show aired. The tape quality was not quite what they had hoped for—it was out of focus, fuzzy, as if something were interfering with their shot. But, you see, it wasn't their fault . . .

Since then Mark has gotten scores of letters from people containing pictures of weird images in the Triangular Field, blurry images, and stories about brand-new cameras with brand-new batteries dying in that field of horror.

There may be an explanation for the animus against cameras and photographers, but logical, skeptical people may not like it.

In one of the seminal books on Gettysburg, author and historian William A. Frassanito may have inadvertently explained what it is that affects photographers and their work in the Triangular Field and Devil's Den areas.

Photographers came to the Gettysburg battlefield after the great conflict to document the slaughter but also to make money. The first photographs of the slain from the Battle of Antietam, or Sharpsburg, were wildly popular with the public, much more so than mere land-scapes of battlefields taken long after they had been sanitized by the burial crews. It appeared to the photographers that the American public, never having seen such a thing before, was ghoulishly hungry for images of dead soldiers.

Frassanito's *Gettysburg: A Journey in Time* analyzes in detail the Civil War–era photos that were taken just after the battle by the several photographers who worked in the field. He has compared the old photos with the present landscape and has identified exact camera sites. In doing so, he has shown where some of the original photographs were purposefully mislabeled by the photographers themselves in order to fill in gaps in the photographic coverage of the battle chronology they intended to portray in their collections. In particular, they labeled Confederate dead from the second day of fighting, lying near the Rose Farm on the south end of the battlefield, as Union soldiers of the Iron Brigade, a unit that fought and died west of Gettysburg on the first day of the battle.

It was not the only ruse they committed. The other was not only misleading, but downright ghoulish.

It was July 6, 1863.

Gardner and O'Sullivan had been photographing all day. The method was tedious. In a portable darkroom, the photographer's assistant prepared a glass "wet plate" covered with a light-sensitive solution and placed it in a light-proof container to take to the cameraman in the field. The cameraman placed it in the camera, removed the container, and exposed the plate for several seconds. The assistant returned it to the darkroom, where it was then "developed" with other chemicals. According to Frassanito, one plate took about ten minutes, from preparation to development. Not exactly "point-and-shoot" technology.

Fortunately, the plates were marked in the field as to their sequence. Also fortunately, one of the finest historians of our generation has analyzed them.

Frassanito is an incredibly meticulous historian. Having been trained by the US Army as an intelligence analyst and assigned to the Joint Chiefs of Staff during the Vietnam era helped hone his exacting methods. In researching his Gettysburg book, he looked at the wet plate negatives in the Library of Congress. He cross-referenced those photographs with field research and took accompanying photos from the exact spot (when 110 years of overgrowth allowed) where the original photographers set up their cameras. He even determined, from the angles of shadows, what time of day the original photos were taken. When he came to analyze the photo of the Confederate sharpshooter behind the wall—the most famous photo to come from the Gettysburg collection—he noticed something strange.

He had seen that soldier before.

Sure enough, the corpse of the young soldier appears in three photos near a large rock about forty yards down the slope of Devil's Den near the Triangular Field. Gardner and O'Sullivan had finished their work and began to walk up the slope when they came upon a neatly piled rock barricade between two large boulders. The natural composition of the site impressed them. Too bad there wasn't a body lying behind the barricade.

It was then that some kind of perverse creativity dawned upon them: Why not "borrow" the body from down the slope, pose him behind the rock wall, and create the romantic illusion of a sharpshooter?

It got worse. Not only did the photographers rearrange this young man's death for their profit, but Gardner made up a story about how he had come back to Gettysburg four months later (to cover Abraham Lincoln's dedication of the National Cemetery and delivery of the Gettysburg Address), returned to Devil's Den, and found a bleached skeleton in a tattered uniform, rusted rifle still leaning against the rock.

So, is it the spirit of this young man—whose mortal remains were dragged from the spot on this earth where his soul left his body to another to fill two photographers' pockets—that causes modern photographers so much grief?

With so many young spirits cast off into the other world in that small space we call Devil's Den and the Triangular Field, it's anyone's guess. But to paranormalists, it's the most likely explanation.

6

STAR-CROSSED LOVERS

Star-crossed romances are not just relegated to literature or TV dramas. There were some real couples whose love seemed to be cursed during the Civil War's bloodiest battle, Gettysburg.

Teenage love affairs weren't any simpler in mid-nineteenth-century America than they are now. In fact, they may have been more complicated. Especially in a small town like Gettysburg, Pennsylvania.

Though Gettysburg is famous around the world for being the site of the largest, costliest battle in the American Civil War, prior to that event it was a sleepy crossroads center for local farmers and merchants to engage in their trades, buy and sell goods, and exchange information. Lives were patterned according to the Germanic stock of the earliest settlers to the area. Names like Weikert, Trostle, Spangler, Culp (or Kulp), Shindledecker, and Kitzmiller were commonly seen (and still are) on letters and packages in the local post office, and the oddities of the Pennsylvania Dutch (originally "Deitsch"–German) language can still be heard among the populace. "Go red-up your room," meaning clean it, from mothers to children; "It's ally-all," meaning it's all gone; and other quaint sayings can still be heard in Gettysburg up to this very day, as they were before the battle.

Prebattle Gettysburgians rarely traveled very far in their entire lifetime. Unless they had relatives who owned a farm outside of town, their business seldom took them outside the borough limits. The outbreak of war, of course, changed all that.

Prior to the Civil War, carriage making was one of the major industries in Gettysburg. Young Wesley Culp was employed by a carriage maker who decided that the competition was getting too stiff and decided to move his business to Shepherdstown, Virginia (now West Virginia). Culp made the momentous decision to leave his hometown and family and follow his trade south of the Mason-Dixon Line. He could never guess just what this decision would cost him, or the ironic circumstances it would engender.

Once in Shepherdstown, the young man from Pennsylvania began to make friends. He joined a local militia outfit called the Hamtramck Guards, which broadened his circle of friends. In the prewar South (and to some extent in the North), militia units were more social organizations—like softball or bowling leagues—than strictly military. It gave the young men an opportunity to dress up in fancy uniforms, perform sharp-looking drills, and afterward have a picnic dinner provided by, of course, the local girls. But by the spring of 1861, when war broke out between the sections of the country, the drills became serious business.

The Hamtramck Guards were soon mustered into the Confederate service as Company B, Second Virginia Infantry Regiment, and brigaded under the stern eye of a former professor from the Virginia Military Institute, Thomas J. Jackson. At First Manassas they would help him earn the nickname of "Stonewall" Jackson and for themselves, "the Stonewall Brigade" for their tenacious style of warfare.

The Stonewall Brigade would continue to make a name for itself in battles up and down the Shenandoah Valley in the spring of 1862, fighting so often and marching sometimes thirty-five miles a day—so far that they and their comrades would be called "Jackson's Foot Cavalry." Summer of that year would find them joining General Robert E. Lee's Army of Northern Virginia in the fighting during the Seven Days Battles in defense of the Confederate capital, Richmond.

It would prove to be a busy year for Wesley Culp and his fellow members of the Stonewall Brigade. They would clash with the Yankees at Cedar Mountain and Second Manassas, then accompany Lee on his army's first invasion of the Northern states. The invasion was stopped September 17, 1862, outside of a little town in Maryland called Sharpsburg (the name used for the battle in the South), near

Antietam Creek (the name used for the conflict by Northerners.) Nearly 23,000 men were killed, wounded, or missing after the dawn-to-dusk fighting, making the battle the bloodiest single day in all of American history.

In December they helped Lee hold off the North's Army of the Potomac from marching onto Richmond by defeating them in the Battle of Fredericksburg, Virginia.

May 1863 saw them fighting that same army just a few miles west of Fredericksburg at Chancellorsville. Although the Confederates won the battle, they lost forever the services of Stonewall Jackson, mortally wounded by friendly fire.

Again they were on the march north along the Shenandoah Valley, fighting battles in places where they had fought before. After another battle near Winchester, Virginia, Culp got word that a wounded Union soldier in a hospital in Winchester was asking about him.

You can only imagine the shock and horror Culp felt walking into a blood-splattered hospital recovery area and finding Johnston "Jack" Skelly, his boyhood chum from Gettysburg, suffering from a mortal wound. They talked for a while, no doubt of happier times as boys in the small Pennsylvania town where they grew up, perhaps of fishing on Marsh Creek by Sach's Covered Bridge, or of rolling hoops down Baltimore Street in the downtown, or maybe of playing hide-and-seek on Culp's Hill, owned by Wes's uncle. Then the talk got solemn. Jack told a surprised Wes of his secret sweetheart in Gettysburg and that he feared his wound would kill him before he could get back to her. Would Wes carry a last message to her if he ever got back to their old hometown?

Of course Wes promised his friend he would deliver the message if and when he ever saw Gettysburg again. But hopefully Jack could deliver the message himself before too long.

Time ran out. Wes had to return to his unit, the famed Stonewall Brigade, for they were to march the next day, continuing their invasion of the North. And Jack Skelly, in a few days, was bound for another, more mysterious venue we will all visit sooner or later.

Culp's march carried him to at least three strange homecomings.

On the march northward from Winchester, Ewell's Corps (of which Culp's brigade was a part) crossed the Potomac at Shepherdstown, Virginia, Culp's adopted hometown. On June 23, 1863, he and the rest of the Stonewall Brigade encamped near a bullet-riddled Dunkard Church outside of Sharpsburg, Maryland, near where they had fought on September 17, 1862. Then after marching through Greencastle and Chambersburg, Pennsylvania, they headed to Carlisle and the US Army barracks there. Within three days, however, they would march back to Fayetteville, Pennsylvania, to camp, reacting to rumors that the Union's Army of the Potomac was somewhere in the vicinity. On the morning of July 1, 1863, they began to march eastward on the pike. As they advanced, ominous noises of combat reached them. Can you imagine Culp's surprise at returning to his childhood home of Gettysburg, Pennsylvania, to fight in a battle, of all things, and as a Confederate?

That night the Stonewall Brigade passed through the town of Gettysburg and encamped a mile east of the town square (or the Diamond, as it was called by the locals) on the road to Hanover.

Their position was at the extreme left flank of the entire Confederate army near one of the large hills to the southeast of Gettysburg. If anyone mentioned it within earshot of Wesley Culp, he could have told them a great deal about it since he had romped across it as a boy. The hill and the large brick house below it belonged to his uncle.

Sitting just a few hundred yards from the borough limits of his old hometown, Culp realized that he could fulfill his dying friend's last wish and deliver the missive from Jack Skelly to his sweetheart in Gettysburg. Sometime that night or more likely the next morning, Culp walked into Gettysburg, no doubt using some of the back alleys and cross streets he knew from boyhood to avoid Union sharpshooters on Cemetery Hill. He visited the home of Jack's girl on Breckenridge Street, but found out from the family that she was not there. She was attending to her sister, who had just given birth in her house between the battle lines. Though the family pleaded, he would not divulge the message to anyone but her—it was that personal. He said he would return later to deliver it, and he went back to his lines.

As a number of men in the Stonewall Brigade would testify after the war, the hill in front of them would become one of the key terrain features of the Union army's fishhook-shaped position—the "barb" of the hook. But when the Stonewall Brigade took its position, the hill was unoccupied by Union troops. It would have been a very easy thing for the Confederates to march to the top, entrench themselves, and command much of the Union lines with Confederate artillery. And, once there, they would be immovable. It was Stonewall Jackson himself who once said, "My men have sometimes failed to take a position, but to defend one, never!"

But their corps commander, General Richard S. Ewell, decided against an assault that night for several reasons: His men were exhausted from the march to the battlefield, they were somewhat disorganized, the terrain before them was unknown, darkness was falling. Those excuses seem valid.

However, his excuse for delaying his assault the next day seemed to have more to do with atmospherics than military logic.

Robert E. Lee, as he rode into town earlier from the west and crested the main ridge named after the Lutheran Seminary, had witnessed something amazing. Two wings of the Union line, north and west of the town of Gettysburg, had imploded, falling back before his troops in near panic as if caught, as one Union commander described it, between two giant shears closing upon them. If there was any concern in Lee's mind as to the huge volume of firing he heard on his ride into Gettysburg after ordering his commanders not to bring on a general engagement, it no doubt evaporated as he witnessed what was clearly a Confederate victory. He saw the troops in blue fleeing through the town and rallying on the hill with the cemetery on it and the ridge that rose to the south of it.

Early the next morning, July 2, after gleaning information from scouts he'd sent out, Lee devised a plan to attack both ends of the Union line simultaneously, dislodge the enemy from their positions, and drive them back into Maryland and hopefully all the way back to Washington, south of Gettysburg. He formulated the plan for the attack on the southern end of the Union line with General James Longstreet. He sent word to General Ewell, on the other end of his line, to attack when he heard the sounds of Longstreet's battle raging.

Longstreet's assault on July 2 was to begin as soon as he got his men into position. Unfortunately for the Confederates, Longstreet did not march his men as hard as Jackson. In a backhanded compliment to both men, word in the army was that Jackson got to the battlefield earlier, but Longstreet got there with all his men. Longstreet, after many hours, finally got his corps into position and began to shell the Union line around three thirty in the afternoon. Within a half hour he launched his infantry assault, crossing the road to Emmitsburg, Maryland, and heading toward sites unknown at that moment, but soon to be written in the bloodstained book of American battles: the Peach Orchard, the Wheatfield, Devil's Den, and Little Round Top.

As the fighting raged on the southern end of the battlefield, Lee waited to hear the sounds of the fighting begin on the other end of the Union line. Ewell, probably because of a fluke of terrain or perhaps the way the wind was blowing that day, claimed he never heard Longstreet's guns. It wasn't until Lee sent a courier to Ewell to directly order him to launch his attack—around seven o'clock—that it finally got underway.

In the meantime, while Wesley Culp and his comrades waited, they could hear ominous sounds coming from the rocky hill before them: picks and shovels digging into the earth, creating formidable trenches—some of which remain to this day; axmen felling trees to build up breastworks behind which the Union troops could fight; others clearing fields of fire before the breastworks so that their rifle and cannon fire could sweep the open spaces as the enemy approached. The men of the Stonewall Brigade knew what the Yankees were up to—they had done it all themselves when they held a position—and regretted the time wasted waiting to take the hill.

So the Confederate attack on Culp's Hill finally got underway in the early evening of July 2. Some Confederates fought their way foot by foot up the slopes of the hill. Others advanced to the summit and walked right into unmanned trenches with campfires smoldering, coffee in the pots, playing cards strewn about. Wary Confederates, in the dusky gloom of the woods, slowly backed away from what they were convinced was a trap.

Actually, Lee's plan was working. All along he wanted to occupy both ends of the Union line with attacks so that they couldn't spare troops to send to their comrades at the other end of the battlefield. Had they attacked earlier, Confederates would have held those Union trenches or continued their attack into the rear of the Union lines. As it was, they were retreating just as the Union soldiers returned, and fighting broke out.

The two sides fought until around eleven o'clock, even with night combat being somewhat of a rarity during the Civil War. After a few hours' rest and with the first rays of dawn, about four in the morning, they began again. At around eight, in one of the assaults on the Union line on Culp's Hill, Wesley Culp was struck in the head by one of the .58 caliber, soft lead, conical bullets they used during the Civil War, called a minié ball. With him died the last private message from Jack Skelly to his hometown sweetheart in Gettysburg. Not that it mattered.

As if to ensure Jack's message would never be delivered, fate sent another of those deadly minié balls on a mission.

At about the same time as Culp was shot, a stray bullet passed through two doors and struck Jack Skelly's girl in the back as she was tending to her sister, who had just given birth, and baking bread for hungry Union soldiers just outside her sister's house between the battle lines.

Her name was Mary Virginia "Jenny" Wade, and she was the only civilian killed in the three-day battle.

7

DUFFY'S CUT

The old Pennsylvania Railroad's Mile 59 marker is near the town of Malvern. Today the railroad holds little of the respect and awe it once did. People do not understand the massive effort that it took to build the railroad. In the eastern half of the nation, most of the railroad's thousands of miles of track were laid by Irish immigrants. The immigrants had nothing and would work cheap. They were frankly easy to exploit, and so they were exploited. But there are few stories that rival that of the people at Mile 59 and the curse that tied them to that spot.

Phillip Duffy was a subcontractor working for the Philadelphia and Columbia Railroad, and in 1832 he had contracted to lay track near Malvern. He was an Irish immigrant himself, and he hired fifty-seven of his countrymen to lay the track. He picked up the crew on the docks of Philadelphia. Phillip Duffy knew that the immigrants were not railroaders, but they were hungry, desperate, and hard workers. They would lay the track or die trying.

Among the immigrants was at least one woman. She, too, was to work at the site. The immigrants found picks and shovels, wheelbarrows, and shabby, leaky tents at the site. They set up the tents, ate the less-than-adequate provisions set out for them, and began work.

Duffy needed the immigrants to literally cut the center out of a mountain for him. Then they needed to lay a railroad bed and track. It was grueling work that drove the men into the ground. All that work was done for twenty-five cents a day and all the whiskey they could hold.

At the same time, cholera was raging around the world, passed through bacteria from person to person. It was a terrible disease that caused diarrhea, violent vomiting, painful abdominal cramps, dehydration, and eventually death for many. There were no drugs to prevent the disease, and few to treat it once the disease was contracted. At the height of the disease, more than eighty people per day were dying of cholera in Philadelphia alone.

In less than six weeks, the cut was made and the track laid. But in the same six weeks, every single one of the immigrants died. Their bodies were laid in a mass grave and covered over. The railroad announced that the poor immigrants had died of cholera—each and every one of them.

For over 178 years the bodies were forgotten in the ground. The area grew wild and abandoned once again. The track is now part of the Southeastern Pennsylvania Transportation Authority's R-5 line. The story of the poor immigrants and the cholera epidemic was nearly forgotten until two men, Frank and Bill Watson, came into possession of some old railroad documents when their grandfather passed away. Their grandfather was a railroad executive and had kept the documents in his possession for a long time.

Frank is a Lutheran minister with a PhD in historical theology. His brother, Bill, teaches in the history department at Immaculata University, in Malvern. In 2002 the brothers found the file and began to go over it. It was a file that had been kept under lock and key by the Pennsylvania Railroad and eventually by their grandfather for many years. Bill thumbed through the file but was brought up short when he read a ghostly tale within it. The story stated that people talked of Irishmen emitting a greenish glow as they danced upon their own graves.

For Bill this story held special significance because two years earlier he and a friend had experienced something eerily similar. It was September 19, 2000, and Bill and that friend, Tom Conner, had just returned from a gig playing the bagpipes for World War II veterans in the Lancaster area. The two men decided to stop at Bill's office at Immaculata University, approximately one mile from the site of the mass grave. At the time neither man thought about the mass grave. It would not be until two years later that the significance of that night would come into focus.

It was late and both men were still in their Gaelic costumes. They had stopped by Bill's office to use the bathroom and grab a quick cup of coffee. They were on the first floor of the faculty building. Conner glanced out the window and froze. "What am I looking at?" he breathed.

Bill followed his friend's gaze and stopped, too. Both men saw three figures with small heads "standing side by side, their legs opened in a V formation and their arms stretched out to their sides" (as Jonathan Valania recounts in a 2010 *Philadelphia Weekly* article). The figures glowed brightly as if with inner light. The two men stared in amazement at the figures. Suddenly they simply winked out and were gone. It took the men a few moments to move, but they did go out and look over the site. They found nothing.

Now, two years later, Bill held a file in his hands that reminded him of that night. Was it possible? Could he have seen the ghosts of the immigrant workers who died of cholera at Duffy's Cut so long ago?

Subsequently, other stories came out. Former residents of the area had long told tales of bobbing lights dancing through the bottom of the cut, where the mass grave was. In fact, a story would surface that told of a man, walking home from the old Green Tree Tavern, who took a shortcut through Duffy's Cut. It was a foggy, warm night, the man later reported. He was walking through the cut when he saw a green glow coming from the area where the immigrants were buried. Slowly the man eased forward, and suddenly a blue fire erupted from the grave. The man stopped to stare in wonder. In the fire were the figures of some men. They jumped and danced above the grave in the darkness. The story was dated September 1832, only one month after the immigrants had died.

But there was much more to come for the Watson brothers. The two men contacted some friends who were in the field of history. The four friends began work to excavate the site, hoping to open the grave and understand the story much better.

Not all the digging was in the ground, though. Old newspapers and census records had to be combed for whatever information they could provide. The paper trail had to be followed to document every bit of the story. But the team stumbled upon something odd. They found information that led them to believe that they needed to look at the October 3, 1832, edition of the local newspaper, but not a single copy was archived anywhere. The team decided that they would certainly be able to find a copy at the Library of Congress. They needed that day's edition because it supposedly contained information that would help document the finding of the dead immigrants at Duffy's Cut. Strangely, that copy of the newspaper, too, had disappeared. It was then that they began to wonder if there was more to the story than just a tragedy of so many people dying of cholera. All the newspaper reports they could locate indicated that only a few of the immigrants had died of cholera, and yet there were railroad documents that indicated everyone had died. Was it a cover-up? If so, what was being covered up?

By now others had begun to hear the story. Other researchers came forward to join the group. Because the project had very little money, everyone worked for free, donating equipment, expertise, and time as needed. This was becoming more than a project; it was becoming a way for the dead to tell their story. The Watsons just did not know what the story would end up being.

As the research continued, the team began to find that some of the data in the railroad documents simply did not add up. Since approximately half of those who contracted cholera in the epidemic survived the disease, how was it possible that every single one of the immigrants had died of the illness? How could that happen? And how could they have all died at just about the same time? If the deaths had been spread out over days or weeks, the bodies would have been individually buried. A mass grave suggested a rapid end for the people.

There is no doubt that cholera was active at Duffy's Cut, because there is record of a request for medical assistance for the immigrants. The request was denied because of fear of contamination, and the small group was quarantined. It is hypothesized that some of the immigrants began to sneak off and leave the area. It's impossible to know why the men left. Were they seeking medical help from outside the area or were they leaving to protect themselves from infection?

What is known is that the remaining people at Duffy's Cut were surrounded by a formal vigilante group and left there to die. The research team believes that approximately ten men left the cut before the locals walled them in.

The team exhumed its first immigrant body in 2009, and it was then that the theories all began to change. The skeletal remains told a much more sinister story. The remains of nine people have been unearthed so far. Each one had a perimortem wound to the skull. The wounds indicate that all these people had the back of their heads crushed prior to death. How did that happen?

The sinister discovery changed how people looked at the story of Duffy's Cut. Were the immigrants murdered to keep them from leaving the quarantine area? Was there another reason they were killed?

The ghosts of Duffy's Cut seem to be haunting the area where they were cursed by crushing poverty and secrets. They have long been seen walking, dancing, and trying to reach out from the dead to break the curse and tell the living of their last days.

Their efforts may not be in vain. "Before we found the first body, we never heard any animal sounds down in the valley, no bird chirping, just an eerie silence," stated Frank Watson in an interview. "After we started finding the bodies, the birds started chirping again." Perhaps the curse is broken.

8

THE ETERNAL
HUNTER

Legends are often born of deed. People remember the essence of the
story although the details grow and twist with time. Perhaps it was
so with the story of Ewicher Yeeger.

The exact date when Yeeger came to America is unknown, but
his story is still whispered on autumn nights, and his curse, one that
he placed upon himself, is remembered by hunters and woods dwell-
ers even to this day.

The Deutsch (German) people began to settle the eastern part
of Pennsylvania in the 1690s. It was an act of bravery to move to a
distant land and try to set up new towns. It was an act of desperation
and hope to try to start again in the wilds of the New World. It was
into this backdrop that a young man came. Ewicher had made the
journey across the Atlantic with many others and had cleared a small
farm. He worked the fields and hunted with his pack of hounds.

The settlers who had traveled with the young man all did likewise. They cleared ground and raised crops. They hunted and smoked
the meat and tried to survive. They worked together in fellowship and
because of necessity. The young man did his part. He helped to build
structures for family and friends. He shared what meats he did not
need with others who could not provide as well. In fact, the young
man became known as a great hunter. He and his hounds would
haunt the fall nights, ranging through the shadowed glades and along
the moonlit hilltops.

For several years the people struggled and gained ground until
a terrible summer befell the small village where Ewicher lived. The

spring came late and was terribly wet and cold. It was hard to get the crops laid in, and when they were planted the cold chilled the seeds, delaying them even further. The thin sunlight barely awoke the seeds, and when at last they burst through the ground, there were heavy rains that drowned the young shoots.

At last the rain stopped, but it was too late to replace the crops and the villagers worried about how they would survive. Grain was a staple of their diet, but there would be little of that this year. They turned to the woods throughout the summer to forage, but that was not an answer either. The wild beasts fought for their share of the berries and fruits, leaving little for the hungry settlers to eat, and even less to be preserved. Whatever could be foraged was gathered, but it was precious little.

Meat would be the answer for the people of the village, they thought. They would hunt and smoke or dry the meats. They would fish and dry the fish—but the streams began to dry up and the sun became brutally hot in the summer. The remaining berries and fruits withered on the vine. And as summer's heat finally let up, the wild game began to leave, too.

By the time that October's cold gave way to November's promise of snow, the wild game was all but gone. Hunger tore through the village. Men walked the woods looking for a rabbit or a deer, but rarely was any game to be had. The young hunter, Ewicher, who was so good at his trade, likewise spent every moment he could looking for game. He had a little better luck, and he brought back and shared what he could. He watched as the women and children of the village became thin and pale. The children no longer played because it was too much effort.

Ewicher began to hunt ceaselessly. He had to spare enough meat to feed his hounds so that they could hunt even more, but not a scrap was allowed to go to waste.

People began to die from hunger. The very old and the very young died first. Each death drove the young man to even more resolve to keep hunting. If only he could shoot a couple buffalo, then the settlers could survive. If only he could help before more people died.

But the people continued to die. Once-supple young women turned into withered creatures. Grasses were dug up from the snow and boiled in soup pots. Everything edible was devoured. Ewicher continued to hunt, and the little game he brought back seasoned broths and thin soups, but it was not enough.

One night Ewicher heard that a young lady he had been sweet on had just died of hunger. He was horrified by the waste of her life and brokenhearted. It seemed to him to be his fault because he could not provide enough to keep her and her family alive.

Ewicher called up his dogs and told the villagers that he was going out for game. This time he was going beyond the familiar mountains. He was not going to stop until he found food enough to feed the village so that no one else would die. The wiser voices in the village counseled him not to go, for he was as weak and hungry as the others, but they did not voice their concerns too loudly. Was it possible that Ewicher could bring back game? It was their only hope, and so they quietly watched as he gathered his dogs and pulled his powder horn and utility bag over his shoulder.

"I'll not be back until I have found game," he assured those assembled to see him leave. "I swear that I'll not stop hunting until I can bring back enough game to feed us all. Otherwise, I'll hunt on through eternity."

Ewicher and his lean baying hounds slid into the darkness and were gone. A faint spark of hope filled the hearts of some of those who watched him go on that cold night, but others believed that Ewicher would die a lonely death deep in the forest—for if there were game to be had, they would have found it by now.

Days turned to weeks and weeks to months, but Ewicher did not return. He never returned, but late each fall people in the eastern part of Pennsylvania listen late at night for the mournful baying of Ewicher's hounds eternally hunting through the forest and sky. Ewicher cursed himself to a never-ending quest for game. If he ever had another name, it was soon forgotten. He became Ewicher Yeeger, the Eternal Hunter, and he hunts on to this day, cursed never to rest.

But Ewicher did not forget the needs of those who lived in the wilds. In 1732 Deutsch colonists settled in the Blue Mountain area. They cleared land and tried to grow crops, but the mountains were hard on the people. Swift rains washed away crops and then late summer's heat parched what was left. The wild game left for more fertile lands, and by late fall the people were beginning to go hungry.

According to tradition in the area, one late October night local folks heard a strange sound. It was the sound of hounds rushing by, but it came from everywhere at once. The snarling, barking, and baying filled the night air. Those who dared to look out their windows saw nothing but swirling shadows and the shape of a great ghostly man running along with a musket in his hand.

In the morning the people ventured out and found that wild creatures were in the fields. The beasts were weary as if driven and dazed as if frightened, but there they stood for the shooting. The men melted lead and began to kill off the beasts until they knew they had enough to feed their families.

Time and again throughout the winter, the people of the Blue Mountain heard the frightful sounds of the hounds and saw the lean shapes of the dogs and their master running through the night sky. Each time the spirits visited, there was game driven in to feed the people. Rabbits and deer stood shivering and waiting to become food for the desperate settlers.

In this way the village survived the terrible winter, and people began to talk about the story of Ewicher Yeeger. What had befallen the people of the Blue Mountain had been so very similar to what had befallen Ewicher's own village. Had he and his pack driven game in to save their lives? If so, then they would offer him gifts of meat, grain, and cloth.

The legend of the Eternal Hunter was secured. Even today poor Ewicher is said to hunt on. The curse he placed upon himself, to hunt forever, has never abated. But from Pine Grove through the Blue Mountain, old hunters whisper a prayer that Ewicher will smile upon them as they hunt for their families and remember the greatest hunter of all.

In German history there are stories of eternal hunters who are spirits or deities and who bless the people with game. When the Germans settled in America, they brought those legends with them. Exactly how they twisted the stories to fit their new home is unknown, but in the rich Blue Mountain area a unique curse was laid and an enduring legend was born, that of Ewicher Yeeger, the Eternal Hunter.

9

RAUSCH GAP

Legends linger in the mountains of Pennsylvania. It is as if they are trapped by the mountains, the enduring people, and the history that still lives there. In the hills of Lebanon County there is an old legend that some say is true and others say is false. It is up to each person to decide what to believe, but the legend does not die.

In 1823 the Dauphin and Susquehanna Coal Company began digging a coal mine on Sharp Mountain in what is today Cold Spring Township. The coal miners needed a place to stay, and so shanties were built to house the workers. Little shanties were bundled together, creating a hamlet that was known as Rausch Gap. It was important that the coal mine be able to move men to where the work was, and the coal to market. In order to solve that problem, the coal mine built a railroad line that ran through Rausch Gap along the waterway into Schuylkill County. The railroad line ran approximately fifty miles.

One of the men who lived in the village at Rausch Gap was hired by the coal mine company to run the switches on the railroad line through the area. It was his job to keep track of when the trains were running and to switch the lines so that there would not be an accident.

One day the switchman died suddenly. His wife was understandably devastated by her husband's death. Her grief consumed her and she could not think beyond the pain she felt. No one thought about the switchman's responsibilities or what it would mean if no one was there to switch the lines to keep the trains running safely.

That afternoon the lines were not switched and two trains collided. One of the trains was filled with passengers. In the wreck some of the passengers were killed and others were wounded. The widow of the trainman was devastated when she realized what had happened. She believed herself to be responsible for the deaths and injuries aboard that train. If only she had been thinking, she could have notified the station before the switches to stop the trains, or she could have notified the coal company to send someone else there. She believed that her grief had cost those people their lives.

In the days that followed, the woman's grief for the loss of her husband paled as she was consumed by guilt for allowing others to die. Night after night she would find herself drawn to walk along the railroad tracks to where the accident had happened. People began to talk about seeing her walking along the tracks carrying a lantern to light her way. Engineers reported seeing her walking along as if in a daze. Some of them reported to the main office what they had witnessed, but the executives in the main office were loath to take any action against the widow. It was their hope that she would in time regain her senses and return to normal.

One night the widow picked up a lantern and began her lonely trek along the railroad tracks. She stopped at the spot where the trains had collided and waited there. She knew very well that soon another train would come along. When she saw the train barreling toward her, she waited until the last moment and then, still holding the lantern, stepped onto the train track. The engineer attempted to stop the train, but he could not do so in time. The widow of the railroad switchman died beneath the wheels of the engine. She must have believed that this was a fitting death for her because others had died at that spot because of her neglect.

For many years after, people walking along the track at night claimed to see the poor widow carrying her lantern and plodding along as she must have done on those many nights before she took her own life. And if that was where the haunting had ended, it would be tragic and poignant, but that is not the end of the story.

It was said that if people encountered the restless spirit of the widow, she would run at them screaming either in grief or anger. If she disappeared before she reached any bystanders, they could pass on unmolested. But if she ran through the persons who witnessed her haunting, it was a sign that they were now cursed. It was said that those she had passed through were cursed to die in a terrible accident of their very own.

The little village of Rausch Gap continued to exist only until the early 1900s, at which point it became a ghost town. The town died in part because the coal mine moved its headquarters to a more prosperous area. But it also died because the quality vein of coal that had been tapped finally played itself out. The coal that remained was difficult to obtain and was of an inferior quality.

In 1945 the little village was razed completely so that the government could build what would become known as Fort Indiantown Gap. The rest of the land around Fort Indiantown Gap was purchased by the Pennsylvania State Game Commission, and various nature trails were placed on the land. The village at Rausch Gap was virtually forgotten except by historians and archaeologists.

The locals did not forget the legend of what had once happened along the railroad in Rausch Gap. There are still stories and whispered legends on Sharp Mountain and people who insist that the railroader's widow still walks along the trail that is now part of the Rails to Trails system in the state. If she does walk there, and if she still accosts those unfortunate enough to meet her, then the curse is still very much alive. And if the curse is still in effect, it might be better not to walk that trail at night looking for the ghostly widow and tempting the curse to fall upon you.

10

THE DEVIL-
BUILT BARN

The Amish farmers of Lancaster have long been known for their
beautiful farms. Large, neat gardens grace the side yards, and the
barns and outbuildings are usually painted pristine white. There are
flowers along the walkways, and everything is picture perfect. It is a
matter of pride for those farmers.

There is an old story about a farmer who felt no such need to
keep his property up. His yard was sporadically clipped, but no
flowers graced the walkways. His outbuildings had sagging roofs and
needed paint, but the worst part of his property was his barn. The
barn was old and dilapidated. Not only did the barn need painting,
but many of the boards needed replacing. Some of them were curled
with age while others had rotted away, leaving gaping holes where
the cold could get in. It was not a safe structure for the livestock, but
the farmer did not care.

The farmer in question was a tightfisted man who cared more
for how much money he could save than for the danger to his stock.
His wife berated him for his slovenly nature and for the danger that
the barn presented. "It's an eyesore," she'd grumble, looking at it from
the window of the farmhouse. "You need to tear it down and build a
new one," she admonished. "It is the worst-looking barn in the county!
Besides that, it is not safe for the livestock. We need a new barn."

The farmer chafed under his wife's words. "Who says we need a
new barn?" he replied. "Why waste money to fix up perfectly good
shelter just for pride's sake? Who is going to pull the money out of
their pockets for this barn? Our neighbors who complain? No, they

want me to find the money, and this would bankrupt us. I won't replace this barn as long as it stands."

Round and round the couple went, arguing about spending the money. In the end the arguments did no good. The farmer's love of money always overrode other considerations.

One afternoon the farmer and his wife had once again fought over fixing the barn. Winter was fast approaching, and the holey barn afforded little protection from the elements. The roof leaked all over, the gaping holes allowed the wind free access, and the damp would eventually make the livestock sick. The farmer had retreated to the barn in question to grumble about the cost of repairs.

"If you want a new barn but you don't want to spend the money, I just might have the solution to your problems." A deep, smooth voice spoke from the direction of the gaping hole where the barn door had once stood.

The farmer whirled around to see a black shadow of a man silhouetted against the light. The man stepped forward and smiled. He was not a tall man, but he was distinctive. He had pale skin and blond hair. His eyes danced with light, and his smile sent a shudder up the farmer's back.

"Who are you?" the farmer gasped. He stepped back involuntarily, as if the man needed more room.

The stranger grinned again. "My name is not important." He waved his hand as if to dismiss such nonsense. "What is important is that you are having difficulties pleasing your wife and the community, who want you to build a new barn." The man glanced around, taking stock of the holes and gaps in the structure. "You do need a new barn, but the expense . . ." The stranger shuddered as if disgusted by it. "I don't blame you for not wanting to part with so much money. But I might be able to help you."

The farmer sighed. "I just don't have that type of money . . ." he began, but the words fell dead upon his lips. The stranger eyed him askance, as if he knew that the farmer had lied.

"That's of no matter. I can get you a fine new barn for free. Are you interested?" The man arched a brow and offered a greasy smile.

All the farmer heard were the words "new barn for free," and he pinned the stranger with a questioning gaze. "No one does something like that for free. What's the catch?"

The stranger again waved his hand dismissively. "It will cost you not a thing while you are alive. All you must do is sign over your soul upon your death, and I will build the new barn tonight."

The farmer was warming to the subject. He did not really believe that anyone could give away their soul, but if this fellow's offer was real, then he might get a lot of work done on a new barn for free. He did not believe that one person could build a barn in one night either, but again, whatever the fellow did would ease his own burden later. "So let me get this straight. You want me to sign this paper you have, and then you will build me a whole barn as big as the one that is already here and you will do it all in one night?"

The stranger nodded. "That is so."

"Will you bring in a large crew?" the farmer asked.

"No, I alone will build the barn. I will do it between sunset and the first crow of the cock in the morning. If I complete my part of the bargain, then I will have your soul." The seductive voice seemed to ease any objections.

The stranger pulled a folded document from his pocket and spread it out on a shelf nearby. "Just sign here."

He produced a pen and the farmer took it in his quaking fingers. All he could focus on was a free new barn. So easy to sign; so easy to hide from everyone. He thought about his wife and the neighbors and how their jaws would drop. He scratched his name on the form.

The stranger smiled broadly and folded the form. "I shall return at sunset to begin work." He paused and turned back before leaving the barn. "Oh, and two more things: You cannot tell anyone about our agreement, and you must keep your wife in the house while I work. I will not complete the barn if she comes outside. Do you understand me?"

The farmer nodded. "I'll keep her inside."

That evening at supper the farmer told his wife that they were getting a new barn. She was thrilled to hear the news. She began prattling on about plans to have everyone over on the day of the barn raising and what she would cook on that day. The farmer held his hand up. "No need for that," he said. "The whole barn will be built tonight and I've already made all the arrangements. The only thing the fella asked me to do was to make sure that we stayed in the house and did not bother him while he worked."

The wife was more than a little surprised to hear that a single man was going to build the entire barn in one night. His request to keep them away from the barn was also very strange. She was sure that no one could build a barn in a single night, but her husband shrugged off her words.

At sunset she and the farmer sat down to dinner. Suddenly there was a raucous pounding and screeching of wood down by the barn. The farmer paid the sounds little attention, although his hand did shake when he forked a piece of meat off the meat platter. He had never heard such pounding and thumping in his life. His wife was less complacent about what was going on. She wanted to look out of the window, but he was afraid even that would be forbidden, and so he told her to keep seated.

After supper the couple prepared for bed. It sounded as though there was an army down there pounding, sawing, and throwing boards. The farmer began to sweat as he realized that the stranger's offer might have been for real. The terrible thought that he had spoken to the Devil began to settle upon him. If the barn was completed by morning, then his soul would go to hell. It had not been a prank or one man's bravado speaking; his soul had been wagered and it sounded as though the Devil might actually win.

The couple went to bed but neither could sleep. Pounding noises from the barnyard and her own curiosity kept the woman awake. Terror kept the farmer awake. He was beginning to think better of the bargain he had made.

In the early hours before first light, the farmer could stand it no more. He turned to his wife and began to sob out his story. He told her how he was tired of being nagged about replacing the barn. He told her about the stranger who had appeared at the barn the previous afternoon, and about the deal that they had struck. He told her, also, that the man building their barn was not a man at all—it was the Devil!

"Foolish man, what have you done?" The woman grabbed her husband's arms and shook him. "All of this because you do not want to spend the money to build the barn you knew we needed. Your foolish, shortsighted love of money might have cost you your soul. Now tell me exactly what bargain you struck. I need to know word for word what was agreed upon."

The farmer sat in the darkness of his bedroom and repeated the conversation verbatim. It was not a conversation that he was likely to forget. "The Devil said that he would build an entire barn the same size as the barn that stood there and that he would do so between the setting of the sun and the first crow of the cock the following morning. And he told me not to tell anyone and that I must keep you inside no matter what."

The farmer looked beseechingly at his wife. "I do not know that there is anything that can be done now. You have married a greedy fool." He sobbed.

The wife threw back the blankets and stood up.

"Where are you going?" Fear shivered through the man's voice. He could not let his wife be harmed because of his greedy ways.

The wife turned back and pulled her black shawl from the foot of the bed. "I am going to save your foolish soul," she hissed. "Now lie still and do nothing. I must hurry."

The farmer's fear was so great that he could do nothing but comply. He lay in the bed as his wife left him.

Downstairs the wife lit a lantern and hurried to the door farthest from the barn. She draped the black shawl over the lantern to block the light. She hurried to the chicken coop and stepped inside. Then she drew back the shawl and held the lit lantern high. The chickens stirred because of the light, and within seconds the rooster rose from his roost and began to crow.

At the first sound of the rooster crowing, the terrible din from the barn stopped. It was as if someone had flipped a switch. The woman only prayed that she had been in time with her trick to wake the chickens early.

The farmer met her at the back door. "What have you done?" he asked.

"I hope I saved your soul," she muttered. "Come, we must see if the cock crowed before the Devil was done or if I was too late."

The first rays of morning light were pouring over the mountains as the couple dressed and then hurried toward the barn. A magnificent new structure stood before them. It looked complete, and both of their hearts sank. They had been too late. Still, they stepped inside, and the thin light of dawn pointed out a flaw in the barn. Only one board was yet to be nailed. One single board had stood between the farmer and eternity. Yet it was enough to keep him safe.

The Devil was furious at the trick the wife played. He placed a curse upon the barn so that it could not be repaired or completed. Many times people attempted to nail on that one last board, but each time they would find the board torn off the next morning, as if someone had done so in a fit of pique. The Devil's curse would not allow the farmer to have a completely finished barn, but the wife had saved her husband and she was content with that.

11

CHICKIES ROCK

Chickies Rock County Park, between Columbia and Marietta, has a fascinating history that stretches from millions of years ago, when a nascent river carved through its quartzite for some two hundred feet, to the Native Americans who first settled the area and named it "place of the crayfish," to the present, when it serves as a playground for recreationalists.

In 1893 an electric railway—a trolley—was built to carry visitors to the magnificent view from the top. It also served to haul children to the amusement park built by the electric railway company. The railway ran for nearly forty years until it was finally abandoned.

Bike paths and walking trails now lead visitors to the sites of interest in Chickies Rock County Park.

But one thing seems to run through its long history, unbidden and dark: the supernatural.

Locals will agree that the view from Chickies Rock is indeed spectacular and that the history and geology of the site are interesting. But along with the beauty, science, and history are tales that encompass the mysterious: legends of curses, ghosts, and strange monsters.

From the earliest Native Americans came whispers of spirits sighted in the area, such as the tale of the lovers' leap. The most popular version handed down involves a young Susquehannock Indian named Wanunga who lived near the rock in his village. He had long admired a young woman from the village called Wanhuita. The young warrior had returned from fighting another tribe. Perhaps the closeness of death in war made him realize his deep feelings for Wanhuita. When he came home from the war, he took his paramour on a walk up Chickies Rock, determined that he would there declare his love to her.

Just as he was about to pour his heart out, she told him that while he was gone she had fallen in love with a white farmer who had recently come to the area. Wanunga was furious and attacked the young woman. Her screams echoed from the rock and reached the farmer, who had waited nearby for moral support when she broke the news to Wanunga.

The young man ran to help her, but was no match for the warrior just returned from battle, now finding renewed strength in his heart-break. He stabbed and then slit the throat of the white man whose intervention had caused him so much pain. He threw the man's body off the cliff. Still burning with the pain of rejection, he grabbed Wanhuita and leapt off the cliff, carrying her to their mutual deaths.

It is no surprise then that some visitors to Chickies Rock County Park have returned with stories of seeing a young white man dressed in colonial-style clothing standing at the point of the rock. Sometimes they are unnerved by the vision of the same young man rushing through the woods. The frightening thing is that he is seen with bloody wounds and a terrified expression, before he disappears into nothingness before their eyes.

Some hikers passing through the area have heard ghostly drums beating a rhythm from Native American times. Many have searched in vain for the source of the sound.

For some who settled in the area, there seems to be a nagging, palpable presence of misfortune and bad luck. In the nineteenth century, an elderly lady was deprived of her land through the Commonwealth of Pennsylvania's use of the law of eminent domain. Apparently, her struggle against the behemoth that was the state consumed her, and when the legal battles were over, she turned to the only source for revenge she knew: the black arts. From the handbook of a famous braucher (folk medicine and spiritual healer), she cast spells and put a curse upon the land from which she had been forcibly removed by the power of the state. Perhaps it is good that the state claimed the land; it's doubtful that anyone could live upon it without feeling her curse.

From the days of the railway, the long-abandoned railbed has become a hiking/biking trail that runs through the 180-foot Point Rock Tunnel. The tunnel is rumored to be haunted by the spirit of a man struck by a train in the tunnel many years ago.

From a former railroad worker comes the tale of the ghost of an old man with a long beard, carrying a staff with a red flag on it. He was seen by the worker on at least three occasions. The man was working the night shift. More than once, he claimed, the ghost saw him and greeted him before it disappeared.

(This, according to paranormalists, is called an "intelligent" or "interactive" haunting, and it may be the most frightening of all ghostly encounters. It is where the ghostly entity actually acknowledges the presence of the living being, speaks to him or her, and seems to want to communicate, one on one.)

In 1969 some teens descended from Chickies Rock claiming they had seen a ghost up there. Word spread and a large number of curiosity seekers—literally hundreds—visited the rock into the late-night hours over that summer. Many walked away disappointed, but others saw a strange mist form near the rock. Its color varied from green to gray. Others saw a house appear on the rock and just as suddenly vanish. The teens who originated the story later confessed that they had made it all up. Their story, though, drew others to the site who then were convinced they had experienced something otherworldly.

According to local legend, a robber buried his loot somewhere in the area. The early Pennsylvania Dutch settlers believed that ill-gotten gains would keep the spirit of the perpetrator earthbound until the booty was returned to its rightful owner. This robber apparently would rather guard his treasure than move on to a better world, since his wraith allegedly haunts Chickies Rock.

And finally, there are the disturbing tales of supernatural creatures who roam the area. They are small, hairy humanoids whose only desire in life is for the luscious apples that grow in this area of

Pennsylvania. They are called albatwitches, Pennsylvania Dutch for "apple snitchers." Susquehannock Indians also described them hundreds of years ago.

Rick Fisher is a local author and paranormal researcher who chronicles the spooky sightings and weird encounters of the Marietta/Columbia/Chickies Rock area along the Susquehanna River. As a researcher he is naturally skeptical of hand-me-down tales of the paranormal that seem to grow more and more fantastical with each telling. One early morning in 2002, however, his skepticism took a hit with an experience he had.

He was driving home on Route 23 near Chickies Rock when he saw in the distance what appeared to be a person walking up the middle of the road. Closing in on the person, he slowed his car. He saw it was smallish, quite possibly a child. His description is that he saw "a stick-thin figure, about five feet tall, covered with hair," standing in the road, illuminated by his headlights. He flipped on his high beams to get a better look, and the hairy creature turned to look at him. Fisher said he saw two yellow eyes staring back at him. In a second the figure simply vanished, dematerializing from the middle of the road before Fisher's eyes.

Never has an albatwitch been captured or killed. Exactly to what species they belong—or even to what world they belong—is an enduring mystery.

12

HELL ON EARTH

We're all familiar with hell's description: Filled with smoking fire and brimstone with extremely high temperatures, it's a place uninhabitable, except to the damned. Philosophers, metaphysicians, and theologians have argued for centuries whether hell is a real place.

Ask central Pennsylvanians and they will give you an address. In fact, there is more than one place they feel qualifies—but Centralia is the top contender.

Centralia was once a coal-mining town of 2,700 inhabitants with streets, houses, stores, churches, and cemeteries. Now it's a smoldering, hell-like wasteland. Some of the streets are buckled. Holes open unexpectedly in the earth and, in at least one case, nearly swallowed a child. Whiffs of smoke waft up from the land like perturbed spirits unsettled with their fate. Only a handful of living souls still abide in the borough.

The small town was lively enough up until 1962. What could have happened to change it into what many people call Hell on Earth?

The first coal mines in Centralia opened in 1856, and others continued to open throughout the Civil War era. Alexander Rae was the mining engineer who had founded the town specifically for coal mining, but in October 1878 he was ambushed in his buggy and murdered by a group of Molly Maguires, militant advocates for the coal miners. The Mollies were extremely active in Centralia during this time period, perhaps a little too aggressive in their targeting of individuals. Disregarding even the sanctity of the priesthood, three Molly Maguires assaulted Father Daniel Ignatius McDermott. Local legend has it that for their actions, he cursed Centralia and foretold that one day St. Ignatius Roman Catholic Church would be the only structure left standing in Centralia. His curse nearly came true.

As part of that area of Pennsylvania, coal mines abound and even exist under some of the inhabited places. Centralia is no exception, with shafts and tunnels that burrow completely under the village. As the mines were emptied of their coal, bootleg miners risked their lives for what little coal was left, initiating the dangerous practice of "pillar robbing": taking coal from the columns that held up the ceilings of the mines. Shafts collapsed into piles of rubble coal beneath Centralia.

In the spring of 1962, as part of a general clean-up project, the Centralia fathers determined that the local landfill was due. The landfill was located in an abandoned strip mine that was found to have never been completely lined with incombustible material, as specified in Pennsylvania regulations. In spite of prohibitions against open landfill fires, five local firefighters were contracted to conduct a controlled burn in the landfill. The reasons for what happened next are up to speculation.

In the old strip mine were holes into abandoned mine shafts, one as large as fifteen feet. Perhaps the wind was blowing the wrong way. Possibly the firemen missed some smoldering embers when they left for the day, because they were called back later to extinguish fires that had rekindled. The fact that a trash hauler may have dumped some hot refuse into the landfill has also been cited as a cause for the fire. Still another theory claims that a mine fire from 1932 that had never been fully extinguished finally reached the seam under Centralia. No one knows for sure. But before long the huge seam of coal beneath the town caught on fire.

Regardless of how the fire started, it continued to blaze, hell-like, unseen, underground for years. Early attempts to excavate and extinguish the fire, with state assistance, were unsuccessful and continued to escalate in cost. It wasn't until 1979, when John Coddington, Centralia mayor and gas station owner, went to check his underground tanks that the fire's extent was discovered. When he pulled the probe from the tank it seemed unusually warm. A thermometer lowered into the tank was retrieved and read an unbelievable 172 degrees.

In 1981 the earth literally opened and nearly swallowed a twelve-year-old boy who was merely walking through a backyard. His cousin snatched him from falling into the 150-foot-deep sinkhole, saving his life. The gases that spewed from the hole registered as lethal carbon monoxide. It made headlines, and the Centralia fire was no longer just a local issue.

Scientists came, measured the gases coming from the underground fissures, and found lethal levels of several toxic gases.

In 1984 the federal government stepped in and offered $42 million to relocate the residents. With sinkholes opening, toxic gases emanating from the ground, and their town literally on fire beneath their feet, a large number of Centralia residents took the government up on its offer and relocated. In 1992 Pennsylvania governor Bob Casey invoked eminent domain on the town, which had the effect of condemning all the buildings there. In 2009 Governor Ed Rendell signed the papers to begin the eviction of the remaining residents.

Most of the buildings are gone now. Streets still crisscross, but some bear large, heat-created cracks and service only abandoned fields and second-growth woods. Gases still rise from the ground, though measurements have determined that Centralia air is no more lethal now than that in Lancaster. Nevertheless, entrance into the borough is restricted to foot traffic and discouraged by ominous signs.

A number of writers have chosen Centralia as the backdrop for spooky novels, and as of 2015, at least one contemporary filmmaker was doing a documentary on the town.

One of the exposed rocks bears this message from a graffiti artist: "Welcome to Hell."

After a lawsuit, as of 2013 eight residents remained in Centralia, allowed to live there for the rest of their lives.

Father Daniel Ignatius McDermott's curse came very near to coming true. Although St. Ignatius church was torn down in 1997, the Assumption of the Blessed Virgin Mary Ukrainian Greek Catholic Church celebrated its centennial in 2011. It is one of the last structures standing in Centralia.

13

THE GOATMAN CASE

"Hello, this is Jonathan Riley. You know my friend Tom Martin. I was calling in hopes that you can help someone I know. You see, I rent a trailer out in the Bellwood area. It used to belong to my mother, but when she passed on I decided to rent it out. Anyhow, I am currently renting the trailer to a young couple, Maggie and Peter Atwater. They have a son, Conner, who is eight years old, and Maggie is pregnant again. I remember meeting you at a lecture you did and, well, I could not think of anyone else who might be able to help them. Please call me at 555-4814. Thank you."

Patty Wilson picked up the phone to dial the caller back. She knew who Tom Martin was. Tom Martin was a fan of her books, and he followed her investigative career, too. She had met Tom years ago, and he often came to her lectures and book signings. He was an older man with gray hair and a soft-spoken manner. He was knowledgeable and it was always a joy to chat with him. She did not recall who Jonathan Riley was, but she was about to.

Jonathan picked the phone up on the fifth ring. He got right to the point. "I think that something is wrong at the trailer I own. Early yesterday morning Maggie called me and said that she had accidentally locked her keys in the trailer. She wanted to know if I might have a set. I went over and unlocked the door. It was way too cold out for her and the boy to be sitting outside.

"When I opened the door I could not believe what I saw. It was like a tornado had gone through the house. The books and knickknacks were off the shelves and many of the crockery things were broken. The curtains were hanging shredded and the furniture was tossed this way and that. I had been to the house to fix a small plumbing problem only the day before, and the house had been clean and neat. In fact, even when I dropped over unexpectedly, the house was always clean and neat.

"Now, Patty, this couple is not the sort to cause trouble. The husband, Peter, works as an accountant in the office of a local department store. His wife stays at home, and they have their son in a private Catholic school.

"Frankly, Maggie seemed as shocked as I was. She started to cry and I helped her into a seat. She is very pregnant and I wasn't sure if it was hormones or something else. That's when she sent the boy to his room and pulled up her shirt sleeve. A long series of scratches ran down her arm.

"I thought for a second it was Peter and this was a domestic abuse situation, but that was not what she said. She told me this crazy story about green eyes that just blinked at her. She heard growling and things started to move in the house the night before. She said that she had been attacked, but she could not see anyone or anything there. Just this invisible something that beat at her. She had struggled to the door and got her son and got out. She didn't remember locking the door. She did not have her purse or keys or anything. There was a key to the car hidden in the wheel well, and she took it and they drove away. Peter was working overnight, getting the monthly figures ready for morning, and so she drove to Wal-Mart and they slept in the car all night. It was lit and there were people and she was afraid. She said that she had called Peter and he was to arrive soon.

"Anyhow, Patty, this girl really needs help. I thought maybe you could do something to assist her. You're the only person I could think of who wouldn't think she was nuts right off the bat. I mean, she might be nuts, but I believe her—I saw those marks and they look like an animal attacked her. Can you help her?"

Patty waited for a moment before she spoke. "I can talk to her and see what happens, but that's all I can promise right now." Patty scribbled down Maggie's number.

Patty dialed the number as soon as she hung up with Jonathan. The girl on the other end of the line sounded frazzled and frightened.

She broke into tears and described the same thing that her landlord had said, but she also stated that they had been seeing a strange black shadow-type figure with horns on its head and what appeared to be goat legs. She had seen it and so had her son. She sounded desperate, and certainly she needed help.

Patty made arrangements to stop over later that day. She then called her partner, Jim Andrews, and asked him to come along. He agreed, and he picked up Patty a little while later.

The trailer sat in a little wooded lane. It had a big porch and lilac bushes around it. There were flowerbeds that would have been pretty earlier in the year. A celery-green minivan was parked along the side.

Patty and Jim knocked on the door, and a pretty young woman, about twenty-nine years old, answered it. She was slightly over-weight, but it was made more obvious by her pregnancy. Her hair was dark brown and shoulder length. Behind her was a pudgy little boy. She smiled in relief and ushered them in.

Patty and Jim sat and chatted for quite a while. They gave Maggie time to get the fear out of her system, and then to begin to trust them. She showed them the long raked marks on her arm, then asked Patty to look at her back. More angry slashes went the length of her back, and there were handprints, but strangely shaped ones.

As they talked Patty began to feel uncomfortable. She was feeling watched, and suddenly she felt that she and Jim were not wanted there. It was time to begin figuring out what was going on, Patty thought. Jim read her cues perfectly.

He stood up and suggested that it might be a good idea if they could walk through the trailer alone, and Maggie agreed. The hope and fear in the poor woman's eyes moved them both. This was the part of their work in the paranormal that meant the most to them. Helping people who were in a desperate situation took special skills, and they had them. Patty held a degree in psychology and was psychic. Jim had made it his life's work to read people. He was good at it, and he knew that this young woman was terrified.

Jim followed Patty into the bedroom at the back of the hall. Her instincts were leading her, and experience told Jim to follow. He took pictures, and in the photos there was a misty figure beside the bed. They looked for angles of lighting or other causes, but could not find any rational explanation for the white mass that was gathering.

Patty felt drawn to the closet of the master bedroom. She slid open the door and out fell a pile of papers. She had spilled a box that had been leaning against the closet door. Patty reached down to pick the papers up and return them to the box. As her hand touched the papers, she heard a faint growl. She froze. Before her she saw a figure that was half goat and half man, with a goat's head.

Patty stayed still. Jim froze, watching her. He knew that something was happening. The look of fear on her face was obvious. She slowly looked upward. The goat-headed creature glared at her. In her mind's eye images burst: Patty saw Maggie and a man she presumed to be Maggie's husband, fighting with an old African American woman. The old woman was shouting and waving her arms wildly as she chanted. The old woman blew dust from her hand into their faces, and then the whole thing went dark.

Patty stood slowly and met Jim's eyes. He was staring at her strangely. "Are you okay?" His voice was husky with concern.

Patty nodded. "I think I understand now. In fact, I know I do. Come on, I need to talk to Maggie. I think the answers are in that box." She pointed to the closet. "These people have been cursed."

Jim stared at her for a few seconds as if trying to grasp the word *cursed*. It wasn't something that happened to people today. It was an old wives' tale or superstition. But he had worked with Patty for years and he trusted her—even when she went way out there.

Patty moved with purpose as she hurried through the hallway. "Maggie," she began, "I need to ask you a few questions. I know that you just moved here for your husband's work, but where you lived before, it was very hot, right?"

Maggie nodded yes and began to answer, but Patty held her hand up to stop her. "Not yet, please," she said. "Just answer my questions."

Maggie nodded again.

"You lived in a basement apartment, and there was an old African American woman there who did not like you and your husband. In fact, she hated you and your husband. She wanted you to move out and threatened you. Am I correct?"

Maggie blanched. "How do you know that? We haven't told a soul around here about what happened there. You're right, but how did you know?"

"Never mind that, Maggie. I think that it's time you told me the story of the old woman. Was she a witch or voodoo priestess or something? I get that type of feeling."

Maggie nodded, sighing. "It all started so simply. My husband and I rented the basement apartment from a Haitian couple. It was the basement of their home and they had remodeled it for additional income. They were really very nice folks. They shared the yard and the pool with us. They made us feel very welcome. That was until the woman's grandmother came to live with them. The older woman did not want them to live with *moun blan* (white people). I think she wanted the apartment herself. Anyhow, the young woman stopped being friendly. She confronted us one night and said that we were rude to her grandmother. We had not been rude. The old woman would rattle bones at us and leave foul-smelling bags on our doorstep, but we just tried to ignore her. Anyhow, it got worse and worse. She began shouting at us when we came home, and we felt less and less like going back to that house. One night she knocked on the door, and when we opened it she blew some sort of powder in Peter's face and screamed at him.

"The man kept apologizing at first, but I guess he got a lot of pressure from his wife, and one day we found a notice on the door saying that we were being evicted. We fought it for a while, but eventually things got so out of hand that we just packed up and left. Peter's family is from this area, and so he found a job here and we thought we'd put the whole thing behind us. Did the old woman send something to hurt us?"

Patty ignored the question. "Is there something in that closet from that time? Documents or letters or something like that? I strongly feel that there are legal papers that are allowing this spirit access to your house."

Maggie shook her head. "No, Peter took all of that stuff and put it in a safe deposit box at the bank. We decided to do that in case there were any other legal problems that came up because of the apartment rental in Florida." She paused as footsteps on the porch interrupted her.

Everyone turned as the front door opened. Peter Atwater walked in. He was a young man of thirty-two who was overweight and beginning to bald. His suit was rumpled and his tie askew. Maggie ran to him and he hugged her close. He had spoken to Maggie while Patty and Jim were on their way to the house, and so he knew who they were.

Peter stuck one hand out. "I really want to thank you for trying to help us. I don't know what to think." Maggie had been picking up furniture and righting the room while Patty and Jim had been working. Now Peter slid a chair back into place and fell into it. "These past few months have just been a nightmare."

Patty smiled sympathetically. "Your wife has just been telling us about what happened in Florida. In fact, I was asking her if there are any legal documents in the master bedroom closet pertaining to the rental property or the legal issues around that property. Maggie said there weren't, but I feel very strongly that there are such papers back there."

"I told her that you put them in the safe deposit box." Maggie settled down on the arm of Peter's chair.

Peter blanched. "Actually, Maggie, I didn't get to open the box yet. I've just been so busy. They are back there in a box in the closet." He looked at Patty. "How'd you know?"

Patty shrugged. "Just a feeling, but what is important is that I want you to get those papers out of the house right away. Jim and I are going to do a cleansing of the house, but you must understand that the old woman in Florida cursed you in some way. She sent a spirit to torment you. We can cleanse the house now, but you must get rid of the papers or else the entity will be able to return. Normally, I'd have you destroy them, but that's not possible, so we'll do the next best thing."

Patty and Jim took out sea salt and holy water and began the process of cleansing the house. They bound out the entity that had been causing trouble and prayed that God would break the curse. Peter removed the documents that afternoon and the family did not suffer any more attacks. Curses are often considered a thing of the past, but for one Pennsylvania family they were all too real.

14

TROTTER'S CURSE

One of the more famous, interesting, and controversial individuals to fight for America's liberty against the British crown was Pennsylvania native Anthony Wayne. Born near the present town of Paoli in 1745, he earned the nickname "Mad Anthony" during the American Revolution; stories about how he received the name are anecdotal and numerous.

That he was bold, brash, and high-strung is without a doubt; that he drank liquor to excess is legendary, and his battles during the Revolutionary War and his actions fighting them speak for themselves. Starting in September 1777 he commanded Continental troops at the Battles of Brandywine and Paoli; in October he fought the Battle of Germantown and wintered with the Continental army at Valley Forge; in 1778 he commanded troops at Monmouth. In 1779 he fought the Battle of Stony Point, one of his finest and perhaps the battle that earned him his sobriquet.

Stony Point outpost in New York sat on a 150-foot-high bluff surrounded on three sides by water. The fourth side of the fortress was a tidal swamp and grassy plain and the only approachable assault route. The fort was well stocked by the British, boasting several cannon, sharpened log impediments called abatis, and six hundred veteran redcoats. In addition, two British gunboats patrolled the Hudson River to support the fort. At first Wayne did not like what he saw. George Washington arrived to personally reconnoiter and thought differently.

Together he and Wayne formed a plan. They realized the assault lanes were open only at low tide and so planned for a night assault. They called for volunteers to become a "forlorn hope," the first to assault, with only axes, to make passage for the rest of the troops. Many brave men volunteered, but only a few were chosen. A feint was planned on the opposite side of the fort with live ammunition to distract the defenders. Finally, the men in the main assault were told not to cheer, call out to their comrades, or even sneeze and, worst of all, not to load their weapons. They must use the bayonet to do their work. According to legend, when Washington discussed his final tactics, Wayne said, "General, if you will only plan it, I will storm hell!" A nearby eavesdropping soldier turned to a comrade and said, "The man is mad!"

This is but one of the several stories as to how General Wayne got his nickname. His actions once the fighting began would certainly confirm his bold, impetuous behavior in battle.

After a grueling march through a hot afternoon, Wayne's men halted for a brief rest. The men quietly tore pieces of white paper into swatches and pinned them to their hats to identify themselves as Americans in the dark. On July 15, 1779, just before midnight, the assault began.

In the distance could be heard the musketry of the feigned attack. The men of the "forlorn hope" were soon at work, hacking passageways through the obstacles. But almost immediately, the main column ran into trouble. Instead of splashing through ankle-deep water, they had to wade through water chest deep. Their splashing soon alerted the redcoats, and cannon fire echoed over the attackers' heads. Once across the water they realized that the British cannon were emplaced so that they could not be depressed enough and their shots flew harmlessly over the Americans' heads.

Moving swiftly up the slope and closing with the enemy, the Continentals displayed a military discipline they did not have at the beginning of the war. The improvement was thanks to the constant drilling of Prussian major general Friedrich von Steuben, who had worked tirelessly on tactical and individual training—especially with the bayonet.

At Stony Point it gave the Americans an advantage. During the fighting Wayne was shot, grazed on the head by a musket ball.

Before collapsing he shouted, "Forward, my brave fellows, forward." He requested that he be taken to a spot where he could die watching his men achieve victory.

As the fort was surrendering, Wayne's litter-bearers carried him into the British inner lines of defense. The exhilaration of his victorious men was apparently enough to convince Wayne he wasn't dying. As dawn came he wrote to Washington of the great victory: "Our officers and men behaved like men determined to be free."

Wayne went on to command troops through the fighting and siege of Yorktown and the surrender of Cornwallis, which ended the shooting war in America.

Peace was not so kind to Anthony Wayne. In appreciation for his service he had been presented with a large plantation in Georgia, but he lost it due to foreclosure. He apparently continued his drinking habits to excess.

After the Revolution he was called back into service by George Washington to command the United States in the Northwest Indian War. Though the British had lost the Revolutionary War, they maintained a presence, alongside the Native Americans, in the Northwest Territory of the Ohio Valley. They had established Fort Miamis as a base. In mid-August 1794 a strong storm (possibly a tornado, not uncommon for that area) blew through and knocked down a large number of trees around the fort. The British sent the Native Americans out to use the fallen timbers (which lent their name to the battlefield) as natural breastworks and fortifications.

Wayne had drilled his men incessantly while near the fort. One of the Indian leaders said, "The Americans are now led by a chief who never sleeps." Wayne also had studied his enemy.

He knew the Algonquin warriors' custom was to refuse to eat before a battle. So he managed to get word to them that he was about to attack, then postponed the attack. This went on for three days. Finally, with his enemy weak from hunger, Wayne launched his assault. The Indians had taken a new tactic (perhaps trained by the British) of lining up shoulder to shoulder instead of fighting as individuals. It was a mistake. When one part of the line broke before

Wayne's well-trained infantry, the rest followed. The Indians rushed back to Fort Miamis with Wayne's men in pursuit. The British refused to open the doors of the fort for their allies, and a large number were killed or captured in sight of the fort. Never again would the Native Americans trust the British or fight for them against the American settlers. The British claims to more American territory to the west were severely hampered by the lack of cooperation from the Native Americans. Wayne's victory at the decisive battle at Fallen Timbers on August 20, 1794, near Toledo, Ohio, ended the conflict with the Indians in the area and ushered in Ohio as a state in 1803.

Like all geniuses, military and otherwise, Anthony Wayne had curses he lived with. One was alcohol. Another was a savage, illogical temper exacerbated by strong drink. No people knew that better than his aides de camp.

In 1792 Wayne was stationed at Pittsburgh. In between fighting Indians, he apparently drank to excess. Who knows what drove him to it? Boredom was probably one of the factors. After the excitement of the life he led during the Revolution, outpost duty was maddeningly dull. Loneliness for his family and home, completely at the other end of the Commonwealth of Pennsylvania, may have been another reason to turn to the demon rum. But when he began to drink, everyone knew to stay away until the bender ended. For one of his favorite aides, John Trotter, in one instance that was impossible. A dire family emergency had called young Trotter from his post, and he needed to ask for leave from Wayne.

Unfortunately, Trotter caught Wayne at his drunkest, protesting some indignity, probably imagined, and fuming at the circumstances. Trotter was as polite as he could be in asking for his leave. It didn't matter. Wayne replied, possibly not even knowing what he was saying by this time, that he did not care what the young man did as long as he left his sight. Figuring it was the best he was going to get, Trotter left immediately for his home and family. Wayne kept drinking.

The brandy must have been in good supply, for, as the story goes, it was several days later when Wayne finally remembered his young aide and called for him. When told Trotter had gone home, Wayne exploded. Cursing Trotter and everyone else in sight, he ordered a patrol to catch up to him and execute him on the spot for desertion. If the patrol members did not, they would suffer the same fate.

Three officers reluctantly left camp to find the young aide and carry out Wayne's distasteful edict.

Eventually the liquor ran dry and Wayne sobered up. Sober, but probably with a terrific hangover, he called for Trotter. Aides told him that Trotter was not in camp and explained the orders Wayne had given the pursuing patrol. Wayne immediately rescinded the order.

It was too late.

Just that morning the patrol had captured the unlucky Trotter, who was read his order for immediate execution and died, no doubt in a quandary as to Wayne's unknowable personality.

Just before he died, he asked for a Bible and chose Psalm 109 to read aloud to his captors: "Wicked and deceitful mouths are opened against me, speaking against me with lying tongues. They beset me with words of hate, and attack me without cause. . . . So they reward me evil for good, and hatred for love."

The arresting patrol no doubt began to squirm as he continued the reading: "May his days be few; may another seize his goods. May his children be fatherless, and his wife a widow. May his children wander about and beg . . . and may his memory be cut off from the earth!"

The men no doubt shuddered at what sounded more like a curse than a biblical passage and hastened with their disagreeable duty. But Trotter continued: "He loved to curse; let curses come on him!" And just before he died, Trotter read one more chilling passage: "May this be the reward of my accusers from the Lord, of those who speak evil against my life."

Quickly, before he could utter another curse, they ended Trotter's young life.

As we all know, curses are mere superstition, believed in only by uneducated, simple folk. But if one source can be believed, Trotter's curse affected not only Wayne, but his executioners as well. In the ensuing years, for their role in the death of an innocent man, one of his killers became a chronic drunk, believing he was being stalked inexorably by a mad dog for the rest of his life. Some came to believe the mad dog he saw was none other than Satan himself, hounding him to death. Another developed diabetes and for the next three decades was plagued by an unquenchable thirst. A third was convinced that multiple devils were possessing him and was considered by all to have gone insane.

As for Mad Anthony: Although his greatest victory at Fallen Timbers lay ahead of his being cursed by John Trotter, he would often wake in the middle of the night to a misty figure forming at the foot of his bed. As it coalesced into human form, he could make it out as the image of his once beloved aide, young Trotter come to visit from the other world and remind him of a rash hour in which military justice miscarried.

And the curse apparently transcended even Wayne's own death.

In 1796, after many hard years of warfare, Wayne died and was buried at Fort Presque Isle in Erie, Pennsylvania. But for years his family in Philadelphia longed to have their hero brought home. In 1809 Wayne's son Isaac was dispatched across the state to gather his father's bones and bring them back to his birthplace for proper burial near the family. Certain that thirteen years buried in the Pennsylvania loam would have decomposed the body, Isaac took with him only a valise in which to carry his father's remains.

Imagine Isaac's surprise when they exhumed his father and discovered a complete, intact corpse inside the coffin. What to do?

After much thought, someone came up with the macabre idea of boiling the flesh from the bones. Isaac concurred, built a huge fire beneath a large cauldron, and stuffed his own father's earthly remains in it. How much time it takes to boil the flesh from the bones of a full-grown human may be answered by the writers of such television programs as *CSI* or—no pun intended—*Bones*. Suffice it to say, the hideous bubbling and cooking must have gone on for many hours, if not days, before the flesh came free from the bones. Poor Isaac then became the target of Trotter's curse as he watched his father's arms, legs, hands, feet, and eventually head pop to the roiling surface and smelled the ungodly odors as the procedure continued.

Finally, the flesh came free of the bones and was reburied, along with Major General Wayne's military uniform, in the grave in Erie from which it had emerged days before. The bones were packed into Isaac's valise on the back of his horse, and he began his cross-state journey to Philadelphia.

But John Trotter's curse didn't end there.

Somehow the lid to the valise came undone. When Isaac arrived home, he and his family were aghast. Half of the late general's bones were not in the valise but had been scattered over much of the Pennsylvania countryside, from Erie to Philadelphia. What was left in the valise was buried at St. David's Church in Radnor.

One theory from paranormalists is that hauntings occur because of an unconsecrated burial. With his bones scattered across Pennsylvania, Mad Anthony Wayne can never rest in consecrated ground. Perhaps this is the reason why a horseman clad in a military uniform of a bygone era is sometimes seen riding, then halting, seemingly searching for something lost on the ground along the route Isaac took in 1809.

Then again, perhaps the spirit of Wayne is doomed to wander the backroads of his beloved Keystone State because of the curse of John Trotter.

15

THE GILDAY CURSE

William Gilday was a prominent businessman in the Stoney Creek area of Dauphin County in the late 1800s. He was a man of principles and firm beliefs, and one of his beliefs was in powwow doctors, also known as brauchers. These were people who practiced Pennsylvania German folk medicine. They used superstition, folk medicine, and magic to heal and help those in need. They also could curse or harm folks when necessary. Usually they did so for money or revenge. Belief in brauchers went hand in hand with Christianity. Many of the incantations and charms were prayers or words from the Bible.

Mr. Gilday had been brought up on a world filled with belief in brauchers, and he was a strong believer himself. He had relied upon brauchers when his family was ill, and he had brought up his children to believe in them, too.

Emma Gilday was a pretty, vivacious young woman in 1878. She was considered quite a catch and not just because she was a daughter of a wealthy man. However, Emma was also a straight-talking girl. She was blunt to the point of almost being rude. She definitely knew her own mind and was not afraid to express it.

One pretty spring Sunday Emma was approached at church by the son of another member. She had known the young man a long time and frankly did not like him. He had asked her to go walking before and she had refused him. He was a persistent young man who did not like to take no for an answer. In fact, he was well-to-do and rarely was denied. He usually could either buy or bully people to get his way. But with Emma it was different. She played hard to get and that only intrigued him. It also made him angry. No one rejected him and got away with it.

On that Sunday morning when he asked Emma to go walking, he did so in a very public way, in front of many of their friends. Emma was exasperated. She tried to gracefully get out of the situation by stating that she was going home with her folks, but the young man did not accept that answer. He pushed her further, and she felt pressured. She again stated that she would not go out walking with him. Going walking alerted the community that a young couple was interested in each other in a romantic way, but she had absolutely no such feelings for this fellow. The young man persisted to the point that others were getting uncomfortable. Emma got up to leave, but the young man grabbed her arm and twisted her back toward him.

"If you don't go with me, I'll visit Mrs. Boyer and have her put a curse upon you. Do you understand me? You'll be sorry you embarrassed me," the young man hissed at her. He viciously shook her. "I'll have her curse you so that you die. You won't be so high and mighty once Mrs. Boyer's done with you."

Emma jerked her arm away and ran toward her parents, who were visiting with another couple in the courtyard of the church. She was crying and disheveled from her tussle with the young man. Her parents knew immediately that something was drastically wrong and quickly made excuses to leave. In the carriage Emma finally let loose with the emotions that were racking her. She told her parents about the persistent young man and how he had threatened her. She caught the look exchanged by her parents when she spoke of his threat to hire Mrs. Boyer.

For the next few days William Gilday worried and waited. He tried to believe that the whole incident would blow over. He had spoken to the pastor and the council, and the young man would be taken to task for his imprudent actions and harsh words. But he could not help thinking that the censure might not be enough. Gilday considered contacting Mrs. Boyer and paying her to leave his daughter alone, but the Bible stated that there should be no communication with witches and the like; surely a woman capable of cursing others should not be communicated with.

As the week passed, the Gilday family fell back into the routine of life. Emma asked to be excused from church the following Sunday, but her father insisted that she attend, for she had done nothing wrong.

Emma feared meeting the young man again and the knowing stares of the others as the story of the previous week's scene was passed in whispers through the congregation. She took pains to stay with her parents and siblings at all times, but she needn't have worried. The church and the community at large had heard the story already and lines had been drawn. Everyone had sympathy for the young woman who had attempted to politely rebuff an unwanted suitor.

Church went without incident, and Emma was relieved when she could close her eyes and let the carriage rock her gently to sleep on the way home. It had been a very stressful morning. She had felt the young man's eyes boring into her from time to time. She had steadfastly refused to meet his gaze. She tried to console herself with the fact that the novelty would be worn off by next week, but she had felt the weight of many people watching her throughout the service.

At home Emma changed from her good gown into an everyday dress to help finish the meal. She was feeling tired and her head was woozy. Her legs felt like lead. Perhaps she was coming down with something, she thought. One of her siblings knocked on the door and told her to hurry up because Mama was waiting. Emma opened her mouth to call out that she was hurrying, but only a harsh yipping sound came out. Emma cleared her throat and tried again, but once more the harsh sound of a dog barking broke the air. Her little sister looked at her in horror. "Stop that, Emmy," she said. "Papa won't like you fooling around."

Emma's eyes were wide and she looked panic-stricken. "I'm not fooling around" was what she meant to say, but what came out were a series of barks. She grabbed her throat and tried to scream, but all that came out was a stringent hissing, like the sound a cat made when frightened.

Emma's sister began to scream, "Papa, Mama, hurry! Something's wrong with Emmy."

Emma heard the pounding of feet upon the stairs and saw her parents burst in with brothers and sisters trailing. She tried to talk again, but once more the barking sound came out. Emma began to cry. Fear, frustration, and uncertainty took over. She clamped her mouth shut. She made a writing motion, and one of her siblings scrambled off to fetch a slate. Emma grabbed it desperately and scratched out. "Can't talk. I can only bark and hiss. Help me, please." She thrust it at her parents, who stared at it uncomprehendingly. Emma barked at them as if to emphasize her point.

Mrs. Gilday grabbed her daughter's shoulders. "Calm down; we must make sense of this. This is not a trick?"

Emma's eyes pleaded for belief. She shook her head no vigorously.

Mr. Gilday placed his hand upon his daughter's back. "Be still, girl, for I believe you. I know what's wrong: That boy must have gone to see Witch Boyer and she has placed a curse upon you. Now all that we can do is try to find a way to break it, for you have been cursed."

Cursed! The word hung in the air as the family tried to absorb it. Emma collapsed on the bed and wept pitifully. Her cries were the only sound in the room for a bit. Mrs. Gilday shuffled the children out of the room and closed the door.

"Oh, husband, to whom do we apply for help? Witch Boyer must be powerful if she can do this to our Emma." Mrs. Gilday sat and held her daughter.

Mr. Gilday sat down on the other side of the bed so that Emma was between her parents. "I do not know, but I shall make inquiries come the morrow. I will find someone and have this curse reversed."

Emma sat up, interested at last in what was being said. She opened her mouth and barked. A stricken look swept across her face, and she dove for the slate that lay on the counterpane. "How long?" she scribbled.

Her father seemed to consider the question. "Perhaps a week or two," he said. Tears slipped from Emma's eyes. "No more than that," he comforted, patting Emma's back. He truly felt helpless to do more for his daughter, but he did know that there had to be help out there and he would find it.

Emma's life changed dramatically after that. Emma stayed in the house for the first few weeks. She left only when her father made arrangements for her to meet with a doctor. Doctor after doctor was contacted. Emma was prodded, probed, and diagnosed, but nothing worked. For three years there was no relief for her in the medical community.

Finally her father had no choice but to rely upon powwow doctors for assistance. She drank draughts of foul liquid, had incantations spoken over her, and carried charms. The strange cures were varied and pointless. None of them worked either.

Even though the family tried to hide the curse, word leaked out. People came to see the girl and find out if it was true. The pastor and the church council came to observe her and pronounced the curse to be valid. The young man who had threatened to curse Emma was sent away by his family for his own protection because tempers were running high against him. His brutish behavior and the subsequent curse of the pretty young girl made him a monster in the minds of many.

Others turned to the Boyer family with hate and anger. How dare Mrs. Boyer do such a foul deed to the young girl? Mrs. Boyer was threatened and her children harassed. The more the Boyers denied having any part in the curse, the more the area people believed Mrs. Boyer guilty. The Boyer house was vandalized, and the family could barely stay in their own home.

William Gilday spent much money and time looking for the next cure. At last he heard of a powwow doctor named Wolf, who he invited to see Emma at their home. The moment Emma entered the room, the man stood up and studied her. He nodded as he said, "Yes, yes, this dear child's been bewitched. It was a wicked and powerful witch that set this curse upon her."

The family had gathered to watch the powwow doctor work upon Emma. They were excited because this powwow doctor was said to be quite strong.

"I will need a basin of clean water," the man stated flatly. He patted a table in the living area. "Place it just here," he said. Emma's mother hurried away to fulfill the request.

Wolf pinned Emma with penetrating eyes. "My dear, I am going to discover who placed this affliction upon you for sure. Once we know who it is, then we shall have the key to breaking this curse."

Mrs. Gilday hurried back with a pan of water that sloshed as she sat it down. She anxiously stepped back and took her seat. Wolf had Emma sit with him as he stared into the water. He instructed Emma to stare intently into the water with him. "I shall pray that God gives us the face of the person responsible for this deed. It shall appear in the water as a reflection and we will all bear witness."

For a long while there was silence. Mrs. Gilday glared when one of the younger children fidgeted. Emma's half sister stared at the water as intently as Emma did. Suddenly the girl gasped, and everyone turned toward the basin and those watching it.

In the still water could be seen the face of Mrs. Boyer. The woman's face was placid. There was no doubting that it was Mrs. Boyer, and Emma's half sister would later publicly state that she saw the face herself and that it was clear.

"And now we have been satisfied," Wolf intoned. "With this information, Mr. Gilday, you should be able to break the curse. I am a discerner, as I told you, and cannot break the curse, but I have given you the likeness of the one who cursed your family. I hope it helps."

Mr. Gilday was thrilled to know for sure that Mrs. Boyer was the guilty party. He had had run-ins with Mrs. Boyer's adult son, who was threatening to sue him for defamation of character, but how could the young man deny what had been witnessed in the basin? Gilday was righteous in his faith that he had the culprit, and word quickly spread of Mrs. Boyer's confirmed guilt.

When Gilday heard that a powerful traveling powwow doctor was in the area, he just knew that he had to talk to the man. The powwow doctor's name was Armstrong McClain, and he traveled the area, preaching and treating those who needed help.

Poor Emma's life had been destroyed by what was happening to her. At times she could talk for a few days at a stretch, but then the barking and hissing would descend upon her and she would be possessed for an indefinite period of time. She would be reduced to writing her words in order to communicate. People in town were kind to her, but she was no longer included in youthful gatherings and no one wanted to walk her home anymore.

Gilday consulted McClain, and the powwow doctor listened intently. He nodded knowingly. "It's a terrible shame what has happened to your daughter," the medicine man stated. "But don't be afraid, because I know what to do." McClain reached into his bags and pulled out a cloth bag. He took a shovel out of his things in his wagon and stepped a little bit away from the wagon. He motioned for Gilday to follow. "I am going to burn this curse away," McClain stated as he dropped a clump of human hair onto the flat part of the shovel and poured a few drops of oil on the hair. McClain struck a match and dropped it onto the hair pile. The hair flamed up and burned brightly, giving off a pungent stink. "Now you must pay special attention on your way home," McClain said. "If you do not see a brindle cow on the way back home, then your Emma will improve by sundown."

With that McClain collected his fee. Gilday was careful on his way home to watch for that brindle cow, but luckily he did not see one. That night Emma did seem better. She said that she felt different and she was able to converse freely. Gilday could not help but feel relief. Perhaps his daughter's life was going to get better.

For some time Emma did well. She'd have small relapses, but they were not long lived at first. Emma eventually met a gentleman and got married. But that was not the end of the curse.

John Boyer, the son of the infamous Mrs. Boyer, was furious at what Gilday and his friends were saying about his mother. The Boyer family was ostracized and harassed. John was worried for his mother's safety and security. The Boyers were considered evil because of the supposed curse.

The curse began to rise up again, and Mr. Gilday once more applied to McClain for assistance. Emma was suffering from the fits of barking and hissing quite frequently again.

This time McClain put together a more showy ritual. He informed the Gildays that there was a ritual he could do, but it would result in the imminent death of Mrs. Boyer, and that after her death her casket would be rent open by the force of her magic leaving her. The Gildays were not deterred by the prospects for poor Mrs. Boyer.

Emma sat and went through the ritual. McClain took a hammer and gently touched both her temples with it. This he called "Killing the Witch."

By now John Boyer had obtained legal counsel and had William Gilday arrested for defamation of character. Gilday was bound over, and there was plenty of evidence that Gilday had defamed the Boyer name. However, John and the rest of the Boyers decided that they just wanted to go on with their lives, and so they moved away.

As for Emma, the ritual did seem to work. She no longer yapped and hissed, but her life would never be the same. Not only did she have the reputation of having been cursed, but she also lost her husband, who died at the age of twenty-eight. Her father passed away in 1884 from apoplexy (what we call a stroke today). Her life appeared to be tainted by the curse that was placed upon the young woman. Poor Emma seemed destined to suffer in her life. Whether she was cursed by an unrequited lover or by fact, this young woman's life was unhappy.

16

THE SERIAL
KILLER'S CURSE

There are places that just seem to bring out the worst in people. Places where bad things just seem to happen over and over again. At first glance the Hawk Mountain Raptor Sanctuary in Kempton, Berks County, seems like a peaceful place. It is a world-class facility that deals primarily with raptors such as hawks and other birds of prey.

But the history of that ground is dark with evil that stretches back in time. Hawk Mountain is perhaps the darkest mountain in the Blue Mountain range, and it seems to have always been cursed.

Before white people ever arrived on Hawk Mountain, it was known as a sacred place. The Native Americans held ceremonies on the other side of the mountain, and they said that spirits walked there. It was a place that was shunned.

White settlers were not so superstitious, and they began to build upon Hawk Mountain. Among the settlers was the Gerhardt family. They built a cabin and began to clear the land for a farm. French and Indian incursions were raging across Pennsylvania at the time, and the Lenni-Lenape who lived in the area sided with the French. They hoped to drive the hated British from their land.

During February 1756, eleven-year-old Jacob Gerhardt was outside in the woods when the Native Americans attacked the family cabin. The boy watched from the forest as his five brothers and sisters and his parents were brutally murdered and scalped and the family cabin was burned. Jacob fled the land in search of help and would go to live with family elsewhere. But as an adult Jacob would return to the land where his family was murdered. He built a stone house that sits upon the mountain to this very day. He lived in the house and raised his family. He began taking in travelers, and the place earned a reputation for hospitality and good food.

In his later years Jacob sold the stone house to Matthias Schambacher and his wife, Margaret. The couple worked to increase the popularity of the inn. During the years that the Schambachers owned the inn, some of the locals began to whisper about strange goings-on there. They talked about travelers who stayed at the inn and were never seen again. The rumors picked up at the end of the Civil War when a peddler stopped at the inn for the night. The peddler was selling Union forces uniforms. A few days after the peddler disappeared, Matthias was seen in a nearby town selling the uniforms.

Schambacher and his wife were not friendly to the locals and so tongues wagged on, whispering rumors and hearsay. They kept to themselves and disdained to socialize with their neighbors. But stand-offishness alone would not have alienated all their neighbors. Those disappearing boarders made more of an impression. Many area folks suspected that the Schambachers got guests drunk, murdered them, and then sold off their goods in nearby towns.

Then there were stories of the strange and delicious sausages that the Schambachers were selling. There was talk about where the meat came from because the Schambachers did not have the livestock necessary to make such sausages. A guest supposedly escaped the inn and told the tale locally of the Schambachers offering him "old German sausage" to eat. The man became suspicious when he realized that there were no pigs or other animals on the property. He did not eat the sausages and snuck out when Matthias and his wife were elsewhere. Local folk believed that the man had narrowly missed being killed and possibly becoming dinner for someone else.

As the stories and rumors spread in the area, folks began to shun the property. They talked of a terrible feeling that seemed to permeate the area around the Schambacher Inn, and some people insisted that their horses would shy and rear up as if spooked when they had to drive them past the inn.

People claimed that there were flashing lights that flared up around the Schambacher Inn at night. Local folks could not help but wonder what caused the flashing lights. Others insisted that there were horrifying screams that pierced the night on occasion. They all agreed that terrible acts were going on up at the inn. The area constable rode up on occasion to question the Schambachers about the supposed goings-on. Old Matthias would scream and threaten the police with lawsuits. He refused to answer any questions.

In the 1870s, when Matthias was on his deathbed, he began to confess his sins in a state of delirium. He told those gathered that he had murdered between eleven and fourteen people. He wept as he told of his terrible deeds. He stated that it was the mountain itself and something evil that walked there that had driven him to murder and madness. Schambacher claimed that the murders were "caused by a great evil that lives on the mountain that whispered to me and urged me to murder."

Matthias Schambacher would be labeled by many as America's first serial killer. Was it possible that something that walked on Hawk Mountain had taken possession of the man and urged him to kill his many victims?

Indeed, there seemed to be some sort of destructive relationship between the mountain, the elements, and whoever owned the ground where the inn sat. As Schambacher's body was lowered into his grave at the New Bethel Church Cemetery, a bolt of lightning struck Schambacher's tombstone. His mourners and those who came to gawk were shocked and horrified by the sight.

After Mathias Schambacher's death the inn remained vacant for over a decade. At last someone purchased the inn. The new owner's name was Matthias, too, but that was where the resemblance ended. This Matthias was a devout Catholic and a good man. This Matthias was kind and loving. He helped people and held prayer services at the former inn on Sundays. He even baptized some of the local children. The inn earned a very different reputation. This Matthias had taken away the taint of murder from the property—at least for a time.

In the summer of 1890, a hiker stopped by the old inn and was shocked to see that the door of the building had literally been torn off. The yard was strewn with furniture, and it was obvious that something traumatic had happened at the house. The pious man was simply gone. The hiker notified the authorities and a search immediately began. For days the searchers continued to look for Matthias. Several days after the good man went missing, his headless body was found in the woods not far from the property. His head was never found. The good man's murder was never solved. It seemed that the spirits of Hawk Mountain had claimed another life.

In 1938 a woman named Ingersoll bought the old inn to use as an office and superintendent residence for the hawk sanctuary. Employees of the sanctuary have reported paranormal events within the walls of the old inn. They report having heard wails or tortured screams from the old house. Others have reported hearing, late at night, a sound like a knife being sharpened. Visitors have reported strange flashing lights in the sky, much like those flashes people reported over one hundred years ago. Nighttime visitors to Schambacher's grave have reported seeing balls of light shooting out of the grave and heading in the direction of the old inn.

There seems little doubt that there is a curse on the land. The natives and early settlers talked about a ten-foot-tall spirit that walked the mountain, and who is to say that he was not real? Would Matthias Schambacher or his victims doubt that the land was cursed? Would the poor beheaded man question the belief that an evil force walked the mountain? The mystery now is whether the ground still bears the stain of the curse. The raptor sanctuary is highly respected, and people flock from around the world to visit its environs. One cannot help but wonder: If the curse has not been lifted, then when will it strike again? And whose life will it take this time?

17

HEX HOLLOW

Visitors to Pennsylvania will see strange, circular, colorful symbols, often painted on the sides of barns, but more often appearing in tourist traps for sale as metal signs, bookmarks, keychains, or other souvenirs. While becoming scarcer outside the Amish areas of the state, they represent a unique folklore, allegedly related to the superstitions of some of the earliest settlers of Pennsylvania. And though we may make fun of what seem to be beliefs of an ignorant nature, when people take them seriously, they can lead to serious, sometimes fatal consequences.

The designs are called "hex" signs and have a symbolic language all their own. Most are for good luck or protection. Others are for prosperity. Signs with doves incorporated symbolize peace and contentment. Those with horse heads protect livestock. Still others symbolize fertility, for crops, farm animals, and people. The signs themselves may not be as old as the Pennsylvania Dutch culture. Some sources say they go back only as far as the early twentieth century, since, prior to that, paint was so expensive that the farmers didn't paint their barns, let alone decorate them. But as paint grew more affordable, the signs as regional decorations began to blossom on barns.

The proliferation of the signs is attributed to one Jakob Zook from Paradise, Pennsylvania, who created the "portable" sign, seen as quaint decoration and a conversation piece in many non-Pennsylvania kitchens. In 1942, as the tourist business began to infiltrate the Keystone State, he created and sold the signs along Route 30, the Lincoln Highway. As the tourist industry in southeastern and south-central Pennsylvania grew, so did the availability of the signs.

But the term *hex* in Pennsylvania Dutch refers to "witch." Hexeria often was used to mysteriously heal the sick using Christian prayer, potions, and physical manipulation. Practitioners were called brauchers or powwow men and women, and they relied on several things for their power. The Holy Bible was ubiquitous during brauchers' ceremonies, as were other esoteric printed sources. Another important book was *The Long Lost Friend*, a collection of herbal remedies and magical prayers by Johann Georg Hohman. Hexeria powers were believed to pass down through generations and grow stronger as they did. Although a good number of people believed in their healing properties, others were convinced that they could be used for evil purposes—thus the term *putting a hex on* someone.

What brauchers did was "try for" their patients. They attempted to help them by giving advice, preparing a love potion, applying a natural substance to a wound or wart, or reciting an incantation that would heal the client.

There is a place in York County that some locals call "Hex Hollow" because of a sinister act brought on by belief in witchcraft. But unlike the Salem witch trials—the 1690s orgy of superstitious hysteria that resulted in the execution of twenty innocent people on the belief that they were witches—this event took place in the enlightened twentieth century.

In the early 1900s Lancaster and York Counties nurtured thriving Pennsylvania German communities with quaint names like Paradise and Bird-in-Hand. Brauchers were important people in these communities, providing social and medicinal services even into this modern period. But for one braucher, his esteem among his neighbors was diminishing.

John H. Blymire was a fourth-generation braucher and thus supposed to have greater powers than his predecessors. But as he got older, he felt his powers growing weaker, his ability to help people diminishing, and thus his status in the community plummeting. In his mind the only reason this could be was that he had been the victim of a more powerful braucher who had hexed him and weakened his powers.

Over the years he blamed any number of people for his fate, including his ex-wife, whom he planned to kill to regain his powers. His plans, fortunately for her, fell apart.

When John "tried for" his clients, nothing happened. After a while they stopped coming to him and he was forced to take work in a cigar factory. He spent much of his wages going to fellow brauchers to determine why his powers had diminished.

At work he met fifteen-year-old John Curry, who asked Blymire for help once he learned that he was a fourth-generation powwow doctor. Curry had problems with an alcoholic father who beat him and his mother regularly and thought the braucher could assist him. Finally Blymire got the respect he sought; Curry got the father figure he needed. Thus a comradeship was born that would, unfortunately, end in murder.

Seventeen-year-old Wilbert Hess was a friend of Curry's, and he and his family were introduced to Blymire. They shared Curry's adulation of the braucher and showed him the *himmelbriefs* they kept in their home. In the lore a himmelbrief was a letter written by a braucher that combined Bible verses and incantations meant to ward off evil from the home. In every room of their home, the Hesses had a himmelbrief across from a picture of Jesus, supposedly to bless and bring good luck to the house. Unfortunately, the himmelbriefs were not working; the family had experienced continual bad luck. The Hesses concluded that a powerful braucher had placed a hex upon them. Further discussion led them all to believe that their hexes both came from the same person.

One evening Blymire visited a powerful, well-known braucher from nearby Marietta, on the Susquehanna River. Nellie Noll was known as the "Marietta River Witch" and confirmed that they had all been hexed by the same person. And she named that person: Nelson Rehmeyer.

To Blymire the mystery was finally solved. He told the Hess family that he had done some work for Rehmeyer when he was younger and had witnessed him go into an underground room beneath his kitchen through a trapdoor. Obviously (to them) it was where Rehmeyer kept his books and performed his braucher's magic. Rehmeyer must have been a practitioner of both white and black hexeria.

Noll had told Blymire that the only way to release the spell of so powerful a braucher was to get a lock of his hair and bury it eight feet underground. They must also take his book of spells and burn it. Blymire would need help, and because the Hesses believed that they, too, were victims of Rehmeyer, they offered their son Wilbert to accompany Blymire and his protégé Curry on a visit to Rehmeyer.

On November 27, 1928, they went to Rehmeyer's farm in the hollow in York County. Rehmeyer was a large man, so at first they merely visited. The next night the men worked up their courage and attacked him, wrestling him to the floor, attempting to cut a lock of his hair. Rehmeyer was apparently more than they could handle, so they bashed in his head with a piece of stove wood and strangled him. To them it was self-defense. After all, he had put a hex on them.

They stole ninety-seven cents from the corpse, then set the house on fire and ran, thinking they had lifted the hex from themselves and the Hess family. Perhaps they did break the hex. But their bad luck continued.

The fire failed to cover the evidence and they were quickly apprehended. The trial, because of its paranormal subject, became international news. Journalists from around the world flocked to cover the superstitious and ignorant people who believed in brauchers, folk medicine, and hexing enough to murder someone over it.

Curry's legal representation blamed his miserable life under an abusive father. Blymire's lawyer produced evidence that he had the mental capacities of an eight-year-old. Hess's attorney offered that the intent was not to kill Nelson Rehmeyer. They were all convicted of murder.

Rehmeyer's house was not consumed by the fire. Soon after the murder the house gained a reputation of being haunted by Rehmeyer's perturbed spirit. In fact, the entire hollow is allegedly haunted and attracts the curious, especially around November 28, the anniversary of Rehmeyer's murder. The house is open periodically to visitors. Some claim to have felt and even seen Nelson Rehmeyer's ghost in the house and hollow.

18

THE STORY OF
REUBEN ROCK

World War II was a time of unparalleled sacrifice and suffering for people throughout America. Families were forever torn apart by the war. Many Americans lost family members overseas, and their bodies were not all brought back. For others their family members returned home in body but not in spirit, or they were mentally brutalized. Some disappeared and some ran away. And some lost their futures or they were forever altered. And for a few life took a dramatic turn toward darkness. So it was for a young couple from Claysburg, Pennsylvania.

Young Rosella Dively and her beau, Reuben Rock, had dated and fallen in love like so many others throughout time. It was a passionate romance, and Reuben had only the best of intentions—to make Rosella his wife. Reuben was also an honor-bound American boy who felt that he had to sign up and help to fight the war. He told Rosella of his intentions and asked her to marry him before he left.

They married and Reuben left. It was an all-too-common story for young couples in that time period. Many sweethearts wed only days before the husband shipped out. Rosella went home to live with a fearful heart and a new wedding ring. She wrote letters when she should have been building her future, and she waited. She waited and prayed and cried, but she could do nothing more, for the world was on fire with hate and her Reuben was out there fighting to stop it all.

Reuben was sent to North Africa, where Erwin Rommel and the Germans were making much headway. He was there for nearly four years. He fought desperately at times and at other times he would find boredom overtaking him. He began to have an interest in the local cultures. He struck up a friendship with some native people and through them was introduced to native magic. What he saw truly intrigued him. Perhaps nothing interested him more than the voodoo doctors. Their exotic rituals and elaborate costumes and ceremonies drew him in. He began learning all he could and participated in rituals as he learned more.

Eventually Reuben fell victim to the brutality of war. He suffered a severe gassing from the German forces. He was carried from the battlefield to a makeshift hospital and from there he received more formal care, but his lungs were badly damaged. Breathing hurt and air wheezed and rasped in his scorched lungs. He could not draw a full breath, and in 1946 he was discharged from the service. He returned home to his Rosella and they began a life together, but it was not the life they had dreamed of.

Reuben struggled to build a cottage for himself and Rosella in their hometown. He built the outer frame of the house and finished only a couple rooms on the first floor before his illness grew so bad that he could not work anymore. He collapsed and Rosella became his nurse as well as his wife.

The couple were very poor because Reuben could not work steadily; eventually he could not work at all. Family and friends tried to help, and Rosella did what she could to manage their situation. She struggled to make food that was nutritious for Reuben and to pay for their basic needs. Rosella cared for her Reuben to the best of her ability.

As his days wound down and both Rosella and Reuben had to admit that he was dying, they talked about the future. Reuben knew that he was leaving Rosella destitute, and that had to have grated on him. Even so, he talked to Rosella about what would happen when he died. He told her over and over during the last few weeks of his life that he blamed the war for his coming death. He felt that the military could have kept him safe, but it had been careless with the men. He was angry and vehement about his feelings.

Reuben made Rosella swear that no matter what, she would not bury him in his military uniform. He wanted nothing to do with anything that was military in nature. Rosella made the promise.

When Reuben returned from the war, he had tried to share with Rosella his experiences in North Africa. He talked about the war only a little, but he talked about North Africa and what he had seen, done, and experienced. He began to talk about the voodoo and the rituals he had participated in, but Rosella grew upset about it. She was shocked about his view of voodoo and horrified that he was messing with what she believed was witchcraft. He took down a metal box that he had brought back from the war and told her that she should never touch it. Rosella was fine with that because she wanted nothing to do with the voodoo and whatever was in the box.

In the final days of his life, Rosella talked to Reuben about his spiritual status. Eventually Reuben asked for a minister and prayed for forgiveness. It was a great comfort to Rosella.

When Reuben died on January 13, 1949, Rosella found herself a twenty-two-year-old widow with a dilemma. She had no money to pay for the funeral. In fact, she had almost no money at all. She really did not know what to do. The American Legion Post 522 sent a representative to talk to Rosella. The organization offered to pay for everything for the funeral, but only if Rosella buried Reuben in his uniform. It had to be a military funeral.

Rosella agonized over the decision. She had sworn to Reuben that she would not bury him in his uniform. However, he had not provided any alternative to pay for the funeral. In the end she pressed Reuben's uniform and instructed the undertaker to dress Reuben in it. American Legion Post 522 arranged the rest of the details. Rosella consoled herself by telling herself that Reuben deserved a military funeral. His sacrifice was just as significant and his death as related to the war as those shot down in the heat of battle.

Rosella grieved terribly for her lost husband. She returned to the little house that Reuben had built for her and tried to continue her life. She lived in the two finished rooms and resolved to move on. But family and friends could not help but worry. Rosella seemed to be fading away. She grew thinner by the day. She told her family that she had no appetite. She could not seem to eat more than a few bites.

Rosella also began to complain that she could not sleep. She said that she heard Reuben upstairs walking around. She confided to her family that she heard something on the roof every time she tried to sleep.

Eventually Rosella's mother had enough of such stories. Her daughter's health was at stake and possibly her sanity, too. Rosella's mother visited the cottage and set out on a search. She found books and papers that told her quite a bit about what her son-in-law had been truly interested in. The books and papers related to African witchcraft and voodoo. They were chilling for the poor woman as she shuffled through them. However, the truly terrifying materials in the metal box were hidden, and Rosella kept her husband's secret.

Rosella's mother insisted that Rosella return to her family home. But even there things grew worse. Rosella grieved terribly for Reuben. She was a shadow of herself. She could not sleep or eat, and she felt tired and listless all the time. She was losing more weight; it was as if something was draining the vitality from her.

One night Rosella finally confided to her mother about the metal box that Reuben had kept, the box he told her to never touch. Rosella explained where Reuben had kept the box, and Rosella's brother was sent to fetch it back to the family house.

Rosella's mother opened the box and tumbled the contents onto the table. An old picture of Rosella fell out. Attached to it was a rabbit's foot. The picture was in a wooden frame. Mrs. Dively took the picture out of the frame, and to everyone's surprise and horror the picture frame suddenly began to move on its own. It crawled in Mrs. Dively's hands, and when she dropped the frame it slithered across the table toward Rosella. Mrs. Dively grabbed the frame and burned it in the fire while the family prayed. She was convinced that Reuben had somehow cursed Rosella or had been cursed by what he had dabbled in while in Africa. By burning the picture frame, she thought that the curse surely had to be lifted.

The story of what was happening to Rosella Rock caught the attention of an area reporter, who interviewed Mrs. Dively. Excerpts from the interview appeared in the *Altoona Mirror*. Mrs. Dively was quoted as saying, "Rosella began worrying about the picture of her that Reuben had carried . . . He was saved in the end, but he had books and things in his house. Rosella was just crazy to be with him. She would probably go to him at any time. That's probably how he did it, by charming her picture that he always carried with him. After he died, Rosie just started wasting away."

For the next few days Rosella seemed to be getting better. She ate more and slept until she finally felt rested. One day she announced that she was doing much better and wanted to return home. Mrs. Dively did not think it was a good idea, but Rosella argued that she needed to get back to a real life. She missed the little home that she and Reuben had built.

Mrs. Dively conceded the point and Rosella packed up to move home to her cottage. The first few nights were relatively quiet. She heard slight thuds on the roof and other sounds, but they were faint and distant and she told herself that it was just the house settling in because it had been left cold for a few weeks.

One night Rosella awoke to knocking on the ceiling of her bedroom. There was no mistaking it. It was the steady pound of a man's heavy fist striking her bedroom ceiling. Rosella was petrified but knew that she had to do something. She slipped from bed and put her robe and slippers on. She hurried up the stairs to the unfinished area above her and looked around by the light of a lamp she had lit. There was no one there, but the pounding still continued. Spooked by what was happening, she hurried back downstairs and nearly dropped the lamp. Looking in the window was a face, a face she had once loved. Reuben was staring through the glass at her. She was sure of it. She stepped closer as if drawn, despite her fear, and he glared at her. It was not an optical illusion; it was Reuben.

Rosella huddled in a chair until first light. Above her head she heard heavy footfalls. From time to time she saw Reuben watching her from the window, and she would put her head down so as not to meet his gaze. How could this be happening?

The next morning an anxious Rosella ran into her parents' home and poured out her horror from the night before. She told them about the knocking and her seeing Reuben in the window. She said that he pounded on the doors and stomped across the roof. It sounded insane, but after what they had already witnessed, they did not doubt her. Still, all that Rosella had now was the house and she had to go back. Her sister accompanied her home that night and they had a tense dinner together. Then the girls climbed into bed together and fell asleep.

Rosella startled awake and felt her sister's hand grab hers. "I heard it, too," her sister whispered. As the pounding on the roof continued, the girls slid out of bed. Rosella's sister insisted that someone had to be up on the roof playing a trick. She told Rosella to stay by the door, and then the sister slipped outside. It was a brightly moonlit night and she could see that no one was up there, and yet the pounding continued. As the girl ran for the door that Rosella held open, she suddenly caught a glimpse of Reuben watching her from the side of the house. There was no doubt that it was Reuben. He glared at the two girls and winked out.

Inside the house Rosella dissolved into tears. "You saw him, too, right? You saw Reuben?" Her breath came in gasps. She was shattered by all that she had been through. "Reuben cursed me," Rosella sobbed. "It's because I buried him in his uniform. I broke my promise to him and he's come back to hurt me."

Each night Rosella suffered the terrible haunting. She had a brother stay with her. She finally returned to her parents' home, but even there they saw Reuben and heard the pounding and thuds of someone on the roof or beating against the outside of the house. Her father and brothers patrolled the property, but they never found anyone living. However, they did see Reuben. He went wherever Rosella was and he haunted her, hounded her.

Mrs. Dively believed that Rosella was right. Reuben had cursed her girl because she had broken her word and buried him in his uniform. Something had to be done before Rosella was driven insane. The poor girl was terrified of what she was experiencing.

Mrs. Dively remembered something that she had seen in Reuben's box along with the picture and frame. There had been papers and some pamphlets in the box. One seemed to nag at Mrs. Dively, and so she took the box back from Rosella and leafed through it. In the bottom of the box there it was, a brochure about a gospel worker and healer named Edward Culp Ferguson. He was a sort of powwow doctor who took on difficult cases. His tract stated that he faced the powers of darkness, and that courage was exactly what Mrs. Dively thought they needed. The man preached and worked all over the area and down into Maryland, but he lived in rural Bedford and that was not far away. The family contacted Ferguson and he came to visit them.

Edward Ferguson was an older gentleman who looked nappy in his suit and tie. An old fedora was tilted jauntily on his head. He had the air of a man who knew what he was doing. He listened to the family pour out their tale. He looked at young Rosella with her haunted eyes and shaking hands and announced that this was a simple problem. He already knew how he would solve the problem. Reuben was upset with Rosella for burying him in his uniform, and the only way to solve the problem was to remove the uniform and perform a cleansing ritual so that Reuben could rest in peace.

Early on the morning of February 22, 1949, Rosella's father and brothers met the gravedigger and Ferguson at the cemetery. The exhumation had been okayed by the local authorities and the church. They exhumed Reuben at seven o'clock and laid his body on a white sheet. The uniform was removed and the body was sprinkled with salt before being wrapped in sheets to be placed back in the casket. Then the body was reburied.

The curse was broken. Rosella never saw Reuben again. The pounding and stomping stopped. In fact, Rosella felt much better. She could eat again and her nerves slowly healed. Edward Ferguson had lifted the curse.

19

THE BABY'S CURSE

Although Helen was only in her early twenties, she had already experienced a great deal of life. She had cared for an invalid brother and mother and been with them both when they died. At the age of fourteen she had run off and married her sweetheart, Chet. She had given birth to three children already and had buried her eldest child. Helen and Chet lived in a poor section of Acosta, Somerset County. They lived in a long row of houses owned by the company that Chet worked for. Their neighbors were mostly immigrants who also worked for the same mining company. Helen had a two-year-old son, John, and an infant daughter named Barbara.

Throughout the past several weeks, Helen had observed a strange trend. She had begun to notice that every time a particular neighbor, Mrs. Connors from down the street, walked by or stopped to visit, Barbara would suddenly burst into violent crying. As long as the woman stayed to visit, Barbara would continue wailing as if she were in pain. The neighbor woman would comment upon what a fussy baby Barbara was. In truth, Barbara was a very happy child most of the time. It seemed that she took to fits of crying only when Mrs. Connors stopped by.

One day Helen was in her backyard hanging laundry when her next-door neighbor, Mrs. Marinari, came out. The woman was an older Italian immigrant whom Helen had become quite fond of. As the ladies both hung the laundry to dry, they chatted about many things. Mrs. Marinari noted that Barbara, who was lying on a blanket nearby, was such a happy and contented baby.

"I know," Helen sighed. "But you know it's the strangest thing: Every time Mrs. Connors comes by to visit, Barbara just bursts into tears. It's almost as though something is jagging her or she has sudden pain. It's been happening for weeks now, and Mrs. Connors always comments upon it. She says that her own baby never fusses but Barbara does. I know it's silly, but it's annoying and vaguely disturbing to me."

The older woman paused in her work to study Helen's face. "This thing that you tell me about, it happens every time she comes to call?"

Helen could hear the apprehension in the older woman's voice, and she paused in her work as well. "Yes, every time she comes it happens. I just don't understand it."

"You may think me foolish," the older woman said, "but I have heard of this before. Back where I used to live there was a woman who could do such things. She would curse children and make them hurt. Sometimes she did it so that their parents would have to pay her money to take the pain away. Sometimes it was done just for spite. With Mrs. Connors I believe that it would be spite. She has put a curse upon the baby and you must take it away."

A curse? Helen could not believe what she was hearing, and yet a thread of dread made her stomach light. As ridiculous as it was, for just a moment Helen had considered the idea.

"Oh, I don't think that such things are possible," she said softly. She was afraid to offend her neighbor, but she was a modern woman and such things were just superstitions from the past.

Throughout the next few weeks, though, things did not get better. Each and every time Mrs. Connors came for a visit, Barbara burst into tears. Worse yet, all the lady had to do now was walk down the street and as soon as the baby laid eyes upon her, she would begin to sob pitifully.

The neighbor's words about curses went round and round in Helen's head. Helen's rational mind argued with a more primal part of her being. Curses were simply superstitions, she told herself, but it was not so easy to believe when Barbara began to cry so hard that it took her breath away. Helen's heart broke for her baby girl, but worse yet was her fear that something was wrong with her baby. She had already buried one daughter, and she could not bear the thought of losing another child.

One afternoon Helen had placed Barbara on a blanket behind some forsythia bushes while she did her gardening. The forsythia bushes shielded the baby from the hot sun and Helen could observe her as she worked. Barbara was playing contentedly for quite a while before she suddenly burst into tears. It was not the normal crying that Helen was used to, but rather the frantic, painful crying that only happened when Mrs. Connors was near. Helen glanced up sharply and met the smirking gaze of the other woman, who stood on the sidewalk. From her vantage point, Mrs. Connors should not have been able to see Barbara.

"Oh my, it must be exhausting to have such a fussy child," the woman commented. "Tsk, tsk," she clucked. "What a shame." The woman continued to smile as if she were truly enjoying the baby's discomfort.

Suddenly fear gripped Helen's heart. It was not rational, but she felt the fear and her instincts took over. She wiped her hands and grabbed up her child. "If you'll excuse us," she said coldly, "I have things to do inside." Barbara continued her wailing until the kitchen door shut behind them. Then, as suddenly as they had begun, the tears ended.

Helen peeked out the window and watched as Mrs. Connors continued to stare at Helen's little house with a strange smile on her face. She stood there for several minutes before moving on.

As soon as the other woman walked off, Helen grabbed her daughter and son and ran for Mrs. Marinari's house. She tried to compose herself before Mrs. Marinari opened the door. Helen told herself to calm down. She'd just pretend that she had stopped by for a visit, and then she'd turn the conversation to the idea of curses and perhaps she could learn more. She suddenly felt compelled to get all the information that she could.

Mrs. Marinari welcomed Helen and the children. She gave John a cookie and fetched him some toys to play with on the kitchen floor.

She clucked over Barbara, who was being her normal self once again, and gave her a toy, too. Then she fixed Helen and herself some tea.

Helen was wondering how in the world she could gracefully get the conversation around to what she really wanted to know. Mrs. Marinari took care of that for her.

"I saw Mrs. Connors standing outside your house again today. She had that 'cat that ate the canary' smile of hers on her face. I could not help but think of what you had told me of the poor baby's reaction. I stepped outside and gave her the eye." Mrs. Marinari made a *V* with her first two fingers and placed it under her eye. "She did not like it and hurried away. I tell you, girl, that woman's up to no good and she is not a good person. You could feel it as she stood there smiling at your house. Did the baby react strangely a while ago?"

Helen could not believe what she was doing, but she poured out the story of what had happened.

Mrs. Marinari nodded as she listened. "I do not mean to frighten you, but this woman has evil in her heart for your child. I do not know why, but there is no doubt in my mind that this is so. You must do something to break the curse."

Helen sighed. "What can I do? I don't even know for sure that anything is really wrong. I would feel terrible if I maligned Mrs. Connors."

Mrs. Marinari leaned forward and took Helen's hands. "There is a way to find out if she has placed the curse," she said earnestly.

"How?" The word propelled Helen into a whirl of fear. Could this really be happening?

Mrs. Marinari spoke softly. "You take a chair and put pins in it so that the sharp ends point up into the cushion. If Mrs. Connors can sit on the pins without discomfort, then she has placed the curse."

Helen shook her head. "I couldn't do that. She could get hurt."

Mrs. Marinari sniffed. "Better her than the little bambina, yes?" She pinned Helen's eyes with her own dark ones. "This you must try. If she gets a little jagged, so what?" Mrs. Marinari shrugged. "But if she don't get jagged, then you have a problem. It is better for you to know."

For the rest of the day Helen wrestled with herself. It was crazy to think that a neighbor had placed a curse upon her child. But if nothing was wrong, why did poor Barbara cry whenever Mrs. Connors was near? It made no sense, but Helen had to know. Mrs. Marinari's words kept echoing in her head: "But if she don't get jagged, then you have a problem. It is better for you to know."

Over the next few days it seemed as if every time Helen looked up, Mrs. Connors was there and Barbara was screaming. When Helen tried to keep Barbara inside, Mrs. Connors knocked on the door and stepped inside to "visit." It seemed as if the woman was seeking her out.

One afternoon after Mrs. Connors had left, Helen found herself turning a kitchen chair upside down. She pried off the backing under the seat and fitted a couple dozen straight pins up through the bottom of the chair. She then tacked the bottom of the seat back in place so that the pins were held firm. Chet would think that she was crazy if he caught her rigging the chair, she thought. She had tried to broach the subject with him, but he had laughed at the notion and suggested that she not visit Mrs. Marinari so much.

Helen righted the chair and gingerly tried to sit on it. The pins jabbed her painfully; she could not lower her weight onto them. She placed the chair in a corner and laid some washing on it. In this way Chet would not sit on the chair and it would be ready when Mrs. Connors came again. Helen had no doubt that she would come and comment upon what a fussy baby Barbara was. It seemed to bring the woman such joy.

Helen did not have long to wait. The very next day Mrs. Connors was knocking upon her door and saying that she had dropped by for only a few moments to visit. Helen felt guilty as she moved the clean laundry and offered the rigged chair to the other woman. She held her breath as the woman sat down, but Mrs. Connors did not yelp or comment in any way. She settled upon the chair and reached out for the cup of tea that Helen offered her. As Helen went through the farce of a visit, her mind raced. "Perhaps the pins have been bent," she thought. There had to be some rational explanation for what had happened.

When Mrs. Connors had gone, Helen once again tested the chair, but the pins were as sharp as ever and she could not sit on the chair. How had the other woman been able to sit comfortably on such a chair? Fear gripped Helen's heart. Was it possible that she had really cursed Barbara? Why?

Helen sought out Mrs. Marinari and told her what had happened. She expressed her fears and concerns. "Why would a woman curse a baby?" she queried as the two women talked softly at the kitchen table.

"The why of it I do not know," Mrs. Marinari said, "but I have no doubt now that this is a curse. You must break it so the bambina is happy once more. Some people are just spiteful. Do not concern yourself with why, but rather with how to end it."

Helen nodded. "But how do I end it? Is there someone I see? Chet would never allow me to spend money on something like this. He doesn't even believe me about this."

Mrs. Marinari sniffed. "Men do not know everything. There are things out there that men don't believe in, but that doesn't mean that they are not real." Mrs. Marinari smiled wryly. "Fortunately you won't have to spend money on this. I will give you a remedy that was once given to me. The next time that woman walks by your house, take a diaper that the baby has peed upon and pinch it between the window and the frame. While you do that, say, 'This curse be gone back where it came from. In the name of Jesus I command this curse be gone.' Then you remove the diaper and wash it." Mrs. Marinari shrugged her shoulders. "It is simple, yes?"

Helen smiled and nodded. The whole thing sounded ridiculous, but what harm would it do? It could be done while Chet was at work.

The next afternoon she got her chance. Barbara was napping on a pallet on the floor while John played and Helen did dishes. Suddenly the baby startled awake, screaming. Helen dried her hands on her apron as she hurried to pick up her baby girl. Her heart nearly stopped when she glanced out the kitchen window to see Mrs. Connors standing in her yard, contemplating the house. "What on earth is that woman doing?" Helen wondered.

An unreasonable fear gripped her. She grabbed John's arm and hurried him toward the stairs. She flipped the lock on the back door on the way. "Upstairs," she whispered. When John tried to protest, Helen hushed him.

She sat upstairs, admonishing the baby and John to be quiet. She could hear Mrs. Connors knocking at the door, but Helen refused to answer. She sat nearly in tears on her bed, huddled up with her babies. She was terrified, and that made her angry.

The minute the knocking stopped, Helen hurried down the stairs. She did not have to look out the window because she already knew that Mrs. Connors was gone. Barbara's crying had subsided into hiccupping sniffles.

Helen felt the fool, but she had saved a wet diaper from earlier in the morning. It was lying on a newspaper on the floor in the corner of the kitchen. She placed Barbara on her pallet and picked up the diaper. She fished in her pocket for the words Mrs. Marinari had told her the day before. She had written them out so that she would not forget them.

Helen opened the kitchen window and laid the diaper across it. She pushed the window down on it until the urine began to seep out. "This curse be gone back where it came from. In the name of Jesus I command this curse be gone." Somehow it seemed anticlimactic. Now all she could do was wait and see.

She pushed the window back up and took the diaper out. She wiped the seal and wall down and put the diaper in the bucket of water to be washed.

For the next two days Mrs. Connors did not come by. Helen wondered if the curse had gone back to her and how she would know it. On the third day Helen was sweeping the porch when Barbara suddenly burst into a screaming howl. At the same moment a shadow fell upon the porch, and Helen caught her breath. She raised her gaze and met Mrs. Connors's amused eyes. "Oh dear, Helen," she smiled. "I do believe that girl of yours must cry twenty-four hours a day. How ever do you get any work done?" Mrs. Connors eyed the small porch stoop critically. "At least you have good reason for things to look so . . . disorganized." The superior tone made Helen's teeth clench.

"Yes," Helen clipped, "at least I do have a reason, unlike some others I know . . ." Helen let the sarcasm drip from her voice. She turned and stepped into the open doorway, taking Barbara with her. "If you'll excuse me, I have things to do." With that Helen shut the door. From the other side of the door came soft laughter. Mrs. Connors was laughing at her. Something about the sound made Helen shiver.

As soon as the children got up from their naps, Helen hurried them outside. She hoped that Mrs. Marinari would be out, and she was in luck. The older woman was picking peas in her garden. Helen allowed John to run down through the common yard toward the older woman and then she picked up Barbara and hurried after him.

The two women chatted briefly before Helen turned the conversation in the direction she needed it to go. She told the older woman that the curse had not been broken by pinching the diaper in the windowsill.

Mrs. Marinari stood, stretching her back, and picked up the bucket of peas. "Come," she said, nodding toward her house with her head. "I think we need something stronger."

Helen wondered what that could be. She sat down and watched John drag out a bucket with a few toys in it. "I don't know if I want to continue this . . ." she began.

Mrs. Marinari pinned her with a severe look. "You want the bambina to cry every time that nasty lady goes by? This cure will surely work. It is old, but I have seen it done before. Trust me."

Helen shrugged. The last cure hadn't worked, but she did not mention that.

Mrs. Marinari pulled a large metal can off the shelf above the sink. She poured out a generous portion of salt into a chipped crockery bowl and plopped it down before Helen. "You listen to me and use this salt. Start in the attic and go around the edges of the room so that you will end at the doorway. Do that down and out through every room. Do the bedrooms upstairs, down the stairway, and each room on the first floor. Work it so that you end at the front door. Toss out the remaining salt so that none remains. That's important. Don't bring any back into the house. Now, while you do this, say, 'In the name of the Father, and of the Son, and of the Holy Spirit I demand that all spirits leave this house. I break the curse upon my child in the name of Jesus.' You say it over and over and over until you get to the door, and then say it as you throw away the salt. You got this?"

Helen pulled the bowl toward herself and nodded. She committed the lines to memory, and when she went home she took the salt. The next day she waited until Chet was gone and the children were napping. She took the salt and went to the attic. She followed Mrs. Marinari's directions all the way through the house. She cast out the last of the salt as she once again said what she had been told to. She felt silly doing it, but she prayed that it would work. Now all that was left was to wait for Mrs. Connors to visit.

For three days Mrs. Connors did not come, and Helen wondered if she knew about the curse and was angry. But still Helen felt better for having done the ritual. Somehow she felt soothed by it. On the fourth day Helen was out hanging diapers in the backyard when she noticed Mrs. Connors observing her from the street. The woman was frowning, as if she were angry about something. Helen realized at that moment that Barbara was playing contentedly upon her blanket and had not fussed at all when Mrs. Connors stopped to observe them. Helen waved and smiled, but the other woman turned on her heel and left.

After that Mrs. Connors did not visit again. She seemed to take pains to avoid the street where Helen lived. Helen was fine with that. She did not care if others believed her; she had her proof that Barbara had been cursed by that nasty woman. She would pass the story down through her family for many years.

20

THE ZOOT
SUIT MAN

In 1954 Peggy was seventeen years old and looking forward to her future. It was the summer that she graduated high school, and in only another six weeks she would be in college. She was planning to study to be a missionary at a college in Tennessee. It was the most exciting thing that had ever happened to her. Her entire life had been spent living in tenant farmhouses and helping her family with the chores and barn work. She had never traveled, never experienced the world. Peggy was going to have her dreams come true, but with a price tag. Her parents simply were not going to be able to assist her financially. Peggy had spent the entire summer working odd jobs. She took in sewing, worked in a local grocery store, and took every babysitting job she could find. It was babysitting that had brought her to the Dunlap house.

Amy and Landon Dunlap lived on the Sellers' farm. They occupied the tenant house and Landon helped old man Sellers run the farm. When Amy's brother, Peter, announced that he was going to get married, Amy called Peggy and asked her to sit with the boys. Amy's brother was in the military and lived in North Carolina, so Amy and Landon were taking a week off to travel there and back. That meant that Peggy would be paid for an entire week of babysitting.

In many old farmhouses in the area, one bedroom could be accessed only by going through another bedroom. It was that way at the Dunlap house. The boys' bedroom was the larger room that opened off the staircase. Peggy's room was much smaller and could be accessed only by going through the children's room. On the first night there, Peggy had locked the outside doors downstairs before going up to bed. As additional protection she also locked the door to the big bedroom that the boys were in. She did so because she would be locked inside with them.

On the third night in the house, Peggy startled awake in the middle of the night. There was flickering golden light in the room, and for one panicked second she thought that the house was on fire. She threw the blankets back and sat up. Her only thought was to get the boys to safety. But in that same second, she saw something that chilled her soul. She froze, sitting on the edge of the bed, as the flickering light continued to dance around her.

At the foot of the bed there stood a man. He was not an ordinary man. His face was cloaked in shadow, but his blue eyes seemed to glow from under the large soft-brim hat that he wore. A waist-length cape was pulled back from his shoulders. She could see that he wore a baggy dark blue striped suit. A gold watch chain and fob dangled from his waist. Peggy would later learn that the suit he wore was called a zoot suit. The smell that accompanied the man was that of brimstone.

Peggy turned around on the bed until she was facing the foot once more. Her back was against the headboard. Fear gripped her as she realized immediately that what she saw was not an ordinary man. She knew in her soul that she was facing Satan himself.

The man leered at her as the flickering light caught his features. She wanted to avert her eyes but she could not. "You will not become a missionary," the man said softly. His voice was deceptively gentle.

"In the name of the Father, and of the Son, and of the Holy Spirit," Peggy whispered as she shuddered upon the bed. Her mind told her that the only thing left to her was prayer, and so she muttered the words over and over again. "In the name of the Father, and of the Son, and of the Holy Spirit, I command you to leave me now!" Her voice was strident as she began to command this man to leave her. Tears coursed down her face, but she paid them no heed.

"Silence!" The figure stomped his foot for emphasis. "You cannot get rid of me now." He shook his arm at her in anger.

Although she felt her throat closing up, Peggy refused to be silenced.

"Enough!" The anger in his voice was enough to make her want to run in terror. But she held her ground because she could not pass him and because the boys in the next room were sound asleep. She could see them through the open door.

The figure rounded the edge of the bed and came toward her. Her voice quivered, but she never faltered. The words of prayer continued nonstop.

"I tell you that you will not become a missionary," he hissed at Peggy. "If you do, I will come for your children. I will curse them and take them and destroy their lives. Fear me, little girl, for I have the power to destroy your family."

"Dear sweet Jesus," she whimpered over and over. It was a prayer upon her lips. The only thing she could think to say was the name of Jesus over and over again.

The entity stepped back as if burned by the very name. "Hear me, girl!" he shouted. "I curse your children, and I curse you. I will take them and destroy their lives."

There was no great flash of smoke as one might expect, but the figure was gone. The flickering light was gone. The scent alone lingered, gagging her. Peggy clawed her way to her feet, running for the doorway. She slammed the door, mindless of the fact that if it were Satan he certainly could follow. She stood between the beds of the two little boys and looked at their breathing bodies. They were okay, and that was all that she could hope for.

She did not sleep for the rest of the night. She fought with herself about what had happened. She was completely sure that she had been awake. It was no dream. Dreams don't smell of sulfur.

By daylight she had wrestled with her thoughts long enough. Part of her wanted to go home and never think about being a missionary again. Part of her felt compelled to resist the fear and pain this being had threatened her with. If her faith could make this thing leave the room, then it would protect her children when the time came.

Twenty-three years later Peggy was a widowed woman with two daughters. Her oldest seemed terrifyingly drawn to the supernatural. The younger one seemed equally fascinated with all things religious. They were good girls. Peggy had to work two jobs to make ends meet, and the girls took up the slack for her. They did the laundry, washed the dishes, and kept the house for her.

The oldest was seventeen and the younger one fourteen when Peggy was forced to move from their home to a rental house. It was a tenant farmhouse, but there was nothing unusual about that. The area was filled with old houses that farmers rented for a second income.

One afternoon when Peggy came home from work, her daughters seemed agitated. The girls asked their mother to sit down because they needed to talk to her. The girls seemed hesitant, but at last they began to tell bizarre stories.

The older girl stated that she had been having a terrible nightmare for the past three weeks. It was the same dream each night. In the dream she climbed the stairs to the second floor of the house. She felt eyes burning into her back as she climbed and forced herself to turn around and look down the stairs. She fully expected that there would be no one standing at the foot of the steps, but in the dream there was someone there. The man had long blond hair that peeked out from beneath the large slouch-brimmed hat he wore. His waist-length cape was thrown back across his shoulders so that she could see his suit. His hands were thrust into the pockets of the baggy blue striped suit. A gold watch chain and fob dangled from his waist. Slowly, he raised his head and she could see his ruined face. Maggots squirmed in his flesh and his blue eyes glowed up at her.

In the dream the girl always ran down the hall and slammed her bedroom door shut and locked it against the creature. But when she turned, the being was standing in the room with a knife in his hand. The girl always awoke as the point of the knife punctured her left shoulder and slipped beneath the collarbone.

It was a terrible dream and certainly something to be afraid of, but there was more to the story than that. The younger girl, too, had been having nightmares. In her dream she saw a man that seemed to be a doctor tending to a little boy. She watched from the doorway in horror as the man pulled a pillow from beneath the child's head and smothered him to death. When the man turned toward her, it was the same figure that the older girl had seen in her dream.

Peggy froze as she listened to the girls pour out their stories. Oh, she knew who that man was. She had known him since she was seventeen years old herself. She had been a missionary but had left the field to marry and have the girls. Those long-ago words in that small bedroom in another tenant house chilled her soul. Satan had come to touch her daughters. He had kept the curse that he promised to put upon them. She made light of the story in front of the younger girl, but later she took the older girl aside and told her the whole story. She cautioned the girls to be aware of what they saw, did, and read. She kept the girls in church until they were adults, and she hoped it would be enough to keep the curse at bay.

Those girls are now adult women who have children of their own. Their children, too, have had visitations from that satanic figure. Usually the visits started at puberty and stayed with them into adulthood. It is a curse that none of them knows how to break. It is a curse that continues to this very day.

21

THE WOMAN IN
THE DRIVEWAY

Saxton is not a well-to-do area. It is dotted with run-down villages and hamlets, including Puttstown, which is located on Route 915 between Saxton and Broad Top City. Outside of the village proper there sat a little old house near Dunning Creek. The house had a horseshoe-shaped driveway, and it was there in the late 1970s that a terrible crime took place.

Sarah had lived in the house at Dunning Creek most of her adult life. Her husband had brought her there as a young bride. She had buried her husband when he died of a heart attack, and she had raised her children in the little house. Through the years the house had fallen on hard times, just as she had. There was scant money for repairs with mouths to feed and bodies to clothe. The house had slowly become run down and old. Sarah felt much like the house looked. She was a poverty-stricken older woman who tried to keep tattered dignity wrapped around herself.

Sarah had always been a good woman. She raised her children to fear God and she rarely missed church despite the fact that she could not drive. None of her children was currently going to church. They were all in their late teens and had fallen away from the church. It was something that grieved her heart, but she would just keep praying for them to see the error of their ways and return to their faith.

One Sunday evening Sarah sat in her good living room, the room where she had never allowed her children to sit, and watched out the window for Jesse to pull in. Jesse was a friend who often took her to church. Sarah watched the clock and was shocked when she realized that it was nearly seven o'clock. Jesse always came at six thirty sharp. They were both in the choir and had to be there early to practice before the services began. "Something must be wrong," Sarah thought.

She got up to let the dog into the back room where it always stayed when she was not home. The dog was acting up, and she could not figure out why. The dog was running crazily through the house barking. She had never seen the little mutt act so upset. Something about the dog's actions put her on edge. It was a frantic barking.

Sarah glanced out the window and sighed. Maybe Jesse had car trouble. Maybe she had overslept. Surely something had happened. Sarah went to the kitchen and dialed Jesse's number. The phone rang and rang, but there was no answer. That surely meant that Jesse was on her way.

Sarah watched out the window for nearly half an hour more. She felt a thread of fear in her stomach. She tried to calm herself, but she could not stop the fear that was beginning to build. From the back room the dog began to howl, and that only set Sarah's nerves more on edge. What was going on?

Finally she decided to call the church office on the chance that someone was back there and could pick up. The phone rang through, but no one answered. She had hoped that someone could look in the parking lot for Jesse's car or check the sanctuary for her.

By now it was after eight, and Sarah could not shake the feeling that something was wrong. She rubbed her arms to warm up. Why was it so cold in the room? It was a cold and snowy evening, but the woodstove was pumping out heat. The heat just didn't seem to be able to penetrate the fear. Something was wrong—something was very wrong!

Sarah stood painfully on her twisted, arthritic legs and went to the phone once more. She knew where her teenage son, Frank, was and she was going to call him. He could check the church parking lot for Jesse's car and drive by her home just to make sure that things were okay.

Sarah had learned long ago to follow her feelings, and now she knew instinctively that she had to find Jesse. Jesse was in some sort of danger.

She got Frank on the phone and explained to him what was going on. Frank, too, had feelings about things, and as soon as he heard his mother's voice her fears became his own. She was right that something was very wrong. He said a hasty goodbye and ran for his old beat-up car.

The car thundered to life, and Frank made a quick tour of the parking lot at the church. Jesse's car was not there. Next he drove the route that she always took down off the mountain to pick up his mother. Nowhere along the way did he see her car broken down. The car was not sitting in the driveway at Jesse's house either, but he stopped and knocked anyhow. A chill ran up his back and started the gooseflesh going on his arms, and it had nothing to do with the night-time cold. The black windows stared silently at him as if to accuse him of not hurrying. He ran back to the car and jumped in. He had to find her. He just had to. He turned the vehicle back toward home.

Sarah was shaken when Frank reported that he could find no sign of Jesse. She struggled to tamp down the fear and knew that Frank was feeling it, too, by the look in his eyes. "It's time to call the police," she announced and resolutely dialed them.

The Saxton police force was small but efficient. The officer on duty took the information but did not seem unduly alarmed. He comforted Sarah by telling her that Jesse had probably gone to visit someone else and had forgotten to notify Sarah that she was not going to pick her up that night. Sarah did not believe him for a moment. The officer, however, agreed to contact the state police after a town policeman had swung by Jesse's home.

Sarah hung up feeling even more frightened and quickly dialed Jesse's number once more. She gave it ten rings before hanging up. It was getting late: The clock confirmed that it was after eleven.

Sarah told Frank goodnight and went to her room, but she did not sleep. A terrible sadness had been creeping over her for the past half hour. She sat in the darkness and wept bitter tears. She could not have said why she felt so sad and desolate, but the feeling overwhelmed her.

At last Sarah forced herself to lie down and close her eyes. Outside there were night sounds and she strained to hear something unusual in them. Once she thought she heard a distant scream, but when she got up and looked out she saw nothing in the shadows that danced at the edge of the woods. A sliver of moon illuminated the wet, cold woods, but she saw nothing else.

The morning dawned cold and icy. Frank took a long time getting ready to go outside. It was midmorning when he went slipping out toward his car. Across the road there was a strip of woods and then a faint dirt road that ran parallel to Dunning Creek for a ways back into the woods. Frank felt restless and walked across the road and started down the little dirt road. His heart froze when he saw the old car. It was Jesse's car, and the front passenger door hung wide open. Frank could not help himself; he slip-slid up to the car. One woman's shoe lay mutely on the floor mat on the driver's side.

Frank ran, screaming, back across the road to his mother. He reported what he had seen and they quickly called the police. The police came and confirmed that it was Jesse's car. They found her tire tracks in the mud along the edge of the road, on the side where Sarah and Frank lived. Sarah sat and watched, stone faced, as the police searched through the woods while a cold drizzle fell. They found no clues and decided that Jesse had to have been transferred to another car.

They postulated that Jesse had been hijacked and abducted by someone when she slowed down to ease around the turn and into Sarah's driveway.

Kidnapped, the cops said, but Sarah could not reconcile herself to that idea. Why would anyone kidnap a poor old woman who barely made her social security last through the month? That just didn't make sense.

The next week moved in a blur. Sarah kept in contact with Jesse's family, but they knew no more than she did.

On Saturday Sarah's older son, Dan, came for a visit. He tried to get over every weekend so that he could help chop wood and fill the coal buckets. It took some of the pressure off Frank, who kept the coal and wood supplied through the week.

Of course the conversation focused on Jesse and her disappearance. Dan shared their opinion that kidnapping a poor old woman made no sense. Who would do such a thing and why? While Frank and Dan worked outside, the snow began to come down at a steady pace that meant business.

It was Dan who suddenly turned toward Frank. "Frankie, did anyone ever search the old playhouse?" His voice was soft and breathy.

Frank froze and nearly dropped the billet of wood he was tossing on his toes. Frank knew exactly what place Dan meant. There was an old cottage up in the woods that was now a falling-down shack. As kids they had played up there despite their parents' stern warning about the danger of the old place. The shack was back in the woods nearly a mile away, and it could barely be seen anymore. Trees and brush grew up around it, and the structure had taken on a sodden brown color that denoted rot. The place was a rabbit warren of little rooms with doors that swung on worn hinges and broken windows that ragged curtains blew through.

"I'd nearly forgotten about that place," Frank responded. "I don't know, but I don't think so. You wanna walk out there?" Suddenly Frank felt almost compelled to go out there. He felt a strange pull toward the old place.

"Yeah, I think we should," Dan said, looking around the woods that edged their little ratty yard. "Maybe some crazy is living out there, and with you and Mom here alone all week, I think we should check it out." Icy snow blew in his face and Dan shuddered. It was getting colder and the snow was beginning to hide the grass.

The two young men hurried to finish their chores. They didn't want to tell their mother anything about their plans. She had to think that they were just going for a walk.

The brothers slipped out of the house on the pretext that it was too hot for them inside. They had heavy boots, gloves, and hats on along with their winter coats, but the wind picked its way through the layers to chill them quickly.

They stepped into the woods, leaving a clear trail in the snow, and began to hurry. There was a sense of urgency that pulled them. Frank felt it the most. Dan was often skeptical of their mother and her "feelings," but Frank was not because he had inherited the trait, too. Now those feelings were pulling him along. He felt a thread of fear ripple through him, and his stomach felt light.

The shack was hidden behind two hills, and in the gray light of the snowy day it was hard to discern its shape in the distance. The brothers ducked behind a stand of trees and hunkered down. "How do you want to do this?" Frank whispered to Dan. The need to whisper was so strong that it was an instinct. What if there was someone hiding in the shack? What if that person was holding Jesse there?

Dan thought for only a second. "I'll crawl up and look in through the front windows, and you go around and do the same in the back. Hopefully the place is empty, but if not, at least one of us should be able to get away and go for help. Now, stay low and move slowly."

Frank hadn't needed the reminder. He felt fear and danger in every fiber of his being. He crawled as he worked his way around the side of the old shack. What if someone was inside there?

Dan crept along, wincing at every snapped branch and crunching leaf. He inched his head above the sill of the living room window but found only old leaves and debris. Breathlessly he worked his way toward the next front window and peeked in there, too.

Frank was beginning to feel a little silly. He popped his head up and found himself staring at a ruined kitchen. A broken cabinet door hung wildly from one hinge, and plaster and lathe shavings were strewn along the floor. Frank crawl-walked forward toward the next set of windows. He popped his head over the windowsill, then slammed himself back to the ground hard so that he did not scream.

Frantically he scurried around the side of the house and hissed to get Dan to turn around. He motioned wildly and Dan crawled in his direction. Frank pointed at the window and crawled toward it. "She's in there," he hissed. "She's dead." He popped his head up to peer in the bedroom again. He did not want to see Jesse, but he had to confirm what he was seeing. Dan rustled up beside him and looked in, too. A near moan escaped him before he looked away. He felt bile rise in his gorge and knew that he was going to be sick.

Jesse lay on a pile of rubble on the bedroom floor. Her blue coat with the sailor's anchor buttons twisted ruthlessly up over her hips. Her girdle, panties, and nylons were twisted and cut away to give access. Her legs were spread and splayed out crookedly. Her head was twisted to the side, and her hands were over her head as if to protect it. Her wrists and throat were badly cut, and blood had frozen on the floor around her. The side of her head had been beaten in. She stared at the boys with one blue eye.

Both boys scrabbled away from the window and took off running. They hit the door of their house, winded and screaming. Soon the police would take over the scene. They hoped that it was all over for their family, but they were wrong.

Early that following spring Sarah and Frank were asked on several occasions about the old woman who was seen standing at the end of their driveway. They were at a loss for an answer, especially when the woman was described: She had short, curly gray hair, wore a blue winter dress coat, and was missing one shoe. She seemed lost or confused. Twice people stopped to see if they could help, but both times the woman had hurried away toward the little house when approached.

At first the family thought that it was a coincidence, but that soon changed. One night one of Frank's female friends came over for a visit. She had brought along her two small children and had kept them up way too late. Frank carried his friend's daughter out to the car and waited while she snapped her son into the car seat. His friend went around to the other side of the car to snap her daughter in as well. As the woman leaned into the car to do up the harness, the door on the driver's side suddenly opened. An older woman wearing a blue coat stuck her head into the car as if to watch what was going on. The friend screamed, and Frank caught a glimpse of blue coat, sailor's anchor buttons, and Jesse's sad face. The friend jumped back and smacked right into Frank as they hurried around to the other side of the car. The driver's side car door swung open a little farther, but no one was there. Then, to their horror, it slowly shut itself. They no longer saw the old woman, but they did see the door moving on its own.

On another occasion a family friend, Burkey, got into a fight with his wife and she tossed him out. The fellow asked Sarah if he might sleep in his truck in her driveway for a few nights until he patched things up with his wife.

It was a cool evening, and he wound the windows two-thirds of the way up. Burkey wadded up a pillow behind himself and tried to stretch out on the bench seat. He drifted off to sleep hoping he'd not have a sore back in the morning. Burkey twisted and tossed, trying to get into a comfortable position. Suddenly he heard a tapping on the driver's side window. Burkey opened his eyes expecting Frank to be outside the door. Instead he saw an elderly woman with short, curly gray hair and a blue coat. The woman looked at Burkey with pleading eyes. There was a faint blue light seeping out of her, like a halo around her. For a second Burkey froze, trying to figure out what he was seeing. The woman reached out and tapped the window again. Her mouth moved but no sound came out. Burkey knew that face and he struggled to remember who she was. Suddenly it hit him: He'd seen her face in a picture that Sarah had shown him. She was Sarah's friend who had been abducted in the driveway, and she was supposed to be dead.

Burkey stared in horror at the woman. Blue-tipped fingers tapped the side window again, and he realized that her fingers were mere inches away from the open window. Burkey scrambled forward, slamming his hands down on the horn. The loud sound ripped through the quiet fall night. Burkey fumbled for the window handle and frantically rolled it up.

Patches of light broke the darkness, and within seconds Frank came stumbling out into the driveway in his underwear and a T-shirt. Burkey clawed at the passenger's side door handle and scrambled out.

"Crap!" he shouted, running for Frank. "Crap, Frank, did you see her?" Burkey's arm shook as he pointed back at the truck.

"Who?" Frank quizzed. He looked in the direction that Burkey was pointing. "I don't see anything."

"She was there, I tell you," Burkey insisted. "That lady your mom used to go to church with. You know, the one who got killed up in the woods."

Frank froze. Was it possible? Was Jesse haunting the driveway? Frank's question would be answered over and over again by other witnesses. Through the years, Jesse appeared repeatedly to family and friends. Frank and his girlfriend saw Jesse one night while talking in his car in the driveway. His sister's children talked about the nice lady who sat in the car with them when their mother went back in the house for something one night. They later identified Jesse from pictures. Jesse had been a kind and gentle woman in life who died a brutal and senseless death. Frank was forever saddened by the fact that she seemed cursed to haunt his family's property. He wondered if she stayed because she had a message to deliver or if the violence had cursed her to remain a ghost forever.

22

SOMETHING WICKED THIS WAY COMES

In 1986 Gail and Ryan were a young couple in love. In December of that year they purchased a mobile home to install on the family farm in rural Fulton County, Pennsylvania. They purchased it used from a family in an adjoining county who had bought the home brand new. They set up housekeeping and started married life. Gail sometimes felt as though she were not alone in the house, but Ryan laughed at her when she voiced her opinion. It would not be until two years after their marriage that Gail gave birth to their son, Jamie. Jamie had a pleasant disposition until he was laid down in his bedroom. Jamie would cry incessantly while he was in the crib. If he slept on the couch, on his parents' bed, or even in the little cradle in the living room, he was perfectly content. He seemed to dislike being alone in his bedroom.

Interestingly, Gail began to notice that Jamie wasn't the only one who didn't like that little room. The cat, Peaches, would not enter the bedroom for any reason. But when Jamie was lying in the crib, Peaches would sit in the doorway and watch over him. The cat would not leave his post for any reason. Gail would sit at the table and watch the cat as it glared into the little bedroom. At times Peaches yowled out his anger as if something was threatening him. The hair would go up at the back of her neck, and Gail would run in and grab Jamie.

Ryan thought that his wife was being silly when she would bring up the stories about the cat. He didn't listen to her when she talked about seeing fleeting black shadows in the house either. He didn't believe her stories about hearing dishes crashing in the kitchen only to find that nothing was out of place when she ran in there. Ryan didn't believe any of her stories, at least not until things began to happen to him, too.

It was a Saturday morning and Gail had been called into work. Ryan was in charge of Jamie, and the two of them had slept in that morning. It was Jamie's crying that woke Ryan; he stumbled out of bed to get his little son some breakfast. As Ryan got up and headed for the kitchen, Peaches was right behind him, and that was when he heard the crash. It sounded as though someone had picked up the entire dish drainer and thrown it on the floor. Ryan rushed into the kitchen fully expecting a mess, but there was nothing out of place.

Ryan fed Jamie breakfast and tried to convince himself that there was some logical explanation for the sound of crashing dishes. He got Jamie dressed, placed him in his playpen, and reached for the boy's favorite toy, Mr. Boos. The toy was missing. Ryan figured that the stuffed toy was probably in Jamie's bedroom. He went to the bedroom and searched, but the toy did not turn up. Ryan checked on Jamie in his playpen and turned around to clean up the breakfast dishes. He froze. Sitting on the highchair was Mr. Boos. How did that get there?

Ryan felt a surge of fear go through him. Maybe Gail was not being hysterical after all. Ryan had begun to believe.

Through the next few months, things continued to get worse. The crashing sounds continued. Jamie grew terrified of his bedroom. He was fine when someone was with him, but when he was alone in the room he screamed the whole time. Jamie was not like that in any other room, just his bedroom. Jamie spent every night either on the couch or in bed with his parents.

Perhaps it was the stress of living in a haunted place, but things between Ryan and Gail began to deteriorate. Ryan was growing hard and mean. He hit Jamie freely and often. Gail and Ryan fought over that constantly.

When Jamie was four, Ryan began complaining about Jamie sleeping with them. "He's too old," Ryan shouted at Gail. It seemed that all they ever did was fight, and most of the fights were about Jamie or about Ryan's father, who owned the farm and believed that meant that he owned them, too.

In order to keep the peace, Gail promised Ryan that Jamie would stop sleeping with them. Gail could see the fear in her son's eyes as she explained the new sleeping arrangements. Gail knew how much Jamie hated the bedroom, so she promised that she would lie down with him until he fell asleep. Jamie was sincerely scared and pleaded to not be left alone in the room. In the end Gail promised to sleep with him a few nights until he was used to the room.

The first couple nights Jamie huddled against Gail in the narrow single bed. Gail slept poorly. On the third night Gail left the closet door open because the water heater was in there and it heated up the closet too much if it was closed.

In the middle of the night, Gail awoke because it was terribly hot in the little room. She rolled over and reached up to see if Ryan had shut the window, but it was open. Cool air blew in but did not seem to penetrate the room. It just made a cool spot by the window. She thought about getting up and getting the fan out of the closet. She flipped on her side so that she was looking into the closet. Suddenly two points of red winked at her. For all the world, they looked like red eyes blinking. Her breath caught and her chest constricted. They blinked again. Eyes. They looked like eyes. Her mind scrambled to make sense of it. A toy? What was it?

The darkness shifted in the closet and Gail felt herself stiffen. The red eyes blinked again, and now she could see that there was a figure—a black shadowy figure moving forward slowly and watching her.

As suddenly as the paralysis had come, it broke, and Gail rolled forward off the bed and grabbed at Jamie in the same motion. She ran through the doorway trailing Jamie's trucks sheet.

She calmed down as she entered the living room and turned to see that the shadowy thing was not following her.

Jamie stirred in her arms and she hushed him as she made him comfortable on the couch. She willed her heart to stop pounding against her ribs and her voice to sound calm.

Jamie went back to sleep, but Gail sat beside her son trying to make sense of what had just happened. Telling Ryan was pointless. He would play it off as a dream or her imagination. Her mind recoiled from the logical answer. Gail had to go back and check out the closet.

Her legs were unwilling to follow orders, but she pushed them forward. She flipped on every light in the living room and kitchen as if it were a talisman against what she had seen.

In the glare of the ceiling light, the little bedroom looked amazingly normal. A stuffed bear watched thoughtlessly from the corner. A pile of toy trucks and little boy clothes lay in another corner. Gail took all of this in instantly, but her focus was on the closet door. It was still open. Gail crept toward the closet and scanned it. Clothes, a muddle of toys, and some shoes in a box on the floor met her gaze. The upper shelf hosted a fan with the cord wrapped around it. There was a bag of clothes and a box of blocks. Nothing was there that could explain what she had seen. Behind the clothes and toys a four-foot-high panel was askew. It was the access panel for the water heater, and it should have been secured by tabs that held it in place, but the tabs were . . . broken, twisted and popped out of the wall. As if something had forced its way out of the bowels of the trailer.

Gail turned quickly away and ran out of the room, pulling the door shut behind her. No sense showing Ryan or telling him about this. Sensible Ryan would give a lame excuse and tell her that she had imagined things. She just knew that Jamie was not sleeping in that room alone again.

Through the next few years, Gail kept her promise. Jamie slept on the couch or in his parents' bed. Eventually she put an extra bed in the main bedroom. Things within the family went from bad to worse. Ryan grew distant and angry. There were many reasons. Ryan's father embarrassed them because the trailer was on his land. He demanded money to let them stay even though it changed the original agreement. Ryan's father also threatened to sell the place out from under them. Beyond that, Ryan seemed to withdraw within himself and hide. He punched the walls and threw things at Gail and Jamie. He threw a shoe at Jamie so hard that it bounced off the bed and struck Jamie in the eye, leaving it blackened.

Jamie took the brunt of Ryan's anger. There were dislocated shoulders, bruises, handprints, and more. One of Ryan's favorite tricks was to hit Jamie on top of the head because no bruise would show.

Throughout all of this, the shadow figure continued to appear. In fact, it got stronger the more the family fought. Gail began to notice that the entity appeared more often as the family disintegrated. One afternoon the entity calmly walked across the kitchen behind Ryan as he screamed and threw things. It paused behind him, as if observing what was going on. Gail grabbed Jamie and ran outside. Ryan did not believe her when she told him what she had seen. It was as though Ryan wanted to deny the existence of the entity.

Through the years, Gail had also learned about Ryan's family and their history on the farm. It only further convinced her that something was very wrong on that land. Ryan's grandmother, Hetty, told her that life on the farm with her husband, Jonathan, had been a long nightmare. Jonathan and Hetty had been married only three years when they were forced by circumstances to move to the little farm. At the time, the area was mostly swampland, and it was only through hard work and sheer willpower that they wrestled a decent little farm out of the swamps. Jonathan had never been a very affectionate man, but shortly after moving to the farm he became angry and hateful. He began to beat Hetty and their two small children. As the years went on, his behavior became ever more perverse. He molested two of their daughters and went to prison for that. He beat the livestock and all the children mercilessly. He beat Hetty so hard that she lost a baby she was about to deliver. That baby was buried secretly at the edge of the garden. Hetty planted a cherry tree there so no one would ever dig up her dead baby.

Hetty always maintained that she did not believe in ghosts, but on a few occasions she admitted that the house was haunted or that the land was cursed. Gail did not know which was true, but she knew that something about living on that farm brought out the worst in men.

Gail would think about Hetty's stories as Ryan continued to spiral downward. Was it possible that the ground was cursed? Was the black shadow that she saw part of that curse? Hetty had said that she and the children had seen a shadow figure in the house, at the barn, and in the fields from time to time. Hetty had insisted to the children that it was an optical illusion, but Hetty believed that it was part of the curse.

By the time Jamie turned ten, things had nearly reached a boiling point. One rainy fall afternoon Jamie, Gail, and Ryan were sitting in the living room watching television. Suddenly the shadow figure stepped out of the wall and walked across the room. It slid out a large bay window at the far end of the room and just disappeared. All three of them sat in stunned silence for just a moment. Gail noticed that when it stepped through the window, it bumped a stand she had a plant on and the plant was quivering as though a physical force had struck it. Whatever this thing was, it could affect matter. The very idea that this thing could touch them or hurt them terrified her.

Gail looked at Ryan with haunted eyes. "Did you see that?" she demanded.

At first Ryan would not meet her gaze, but slowly he brought his eyes up to meet hers. "Something wicked this way comes," he muttered. It was a quote from Shakespeare's *Macbeth*. Ryan had seen the shadow man, too. He finally had to admit it.

Two years later Gail gave birth to her second son, and two years after that she gave birth to yet another. It is hard to give up all hope when you love someone, but by the time her third son was two years old she realized that Ryan would never change. He began to abuse the third child, too. One day she waited until Ryan had gone to work, and then she packed what she could carry and what she would need in the station wagon and put the boys in their seats. She drove away with the money she had saved from her job in her pocketbook and nowhere to go.

There is a strange thing about abused children. They often will choose their abuser in a desperate bid to please that person. During the court process that followed his parents' separation, Jamie chose to return to his father and live with him. Gail's heart broke and she was terrified about what would happen. She had wrestled guns away from Ryan when he threatened to shoot Jamie. She had seen Ryan try to strangle Jamie, stopping only because she beat on his back until she broke his grip. She told all of this to the court officials, but there was no proof and they did not believe her. Fear engulfed her as she watched her son go into the world of anger and pain she had tried so desperately to get him out of.

For several months things bumped along. Jamie was angry and hurt by everything that had happened to him and also by the coming divorce. He sided with his father in an attempt to curry favor. He often did not come to see his mother when there was visitation, but he would call her and tell her that he needed money for food or that he needed clothing. His father was providing neither.

It was nearly two in the morning when the shrill ringing of the telephone brought Gail awake. She glanced at the caller ID and it made her heart skip a beat. It was the old home number, and nobody called at two in the morning with good news. A thousand horrible possibilities ran through her head. Had Ryan hurt or killed Jamie? Almost as bad, had Jamie finally snapped and killed his father? Gail snatched the phone from its cradle and said hello. On the other end she heard Ryan's breathing.

"Get over here right now and get Jamie," he exclaimed. "I mean right now!"

"What happened?" she demanded. It was all she could do to keep the fear from swallowing her up.

"I don't want to talk about it. I'll tell you when you get here. Just hurry." The telephone clicked dead.

Gail shrugged into her clothes from the day before as fast as she humanly could. She woke both the babies and got them dressed and tucked into their car seats. It had not escaped her attention that this could very well be a ploy for Ryan to get her back to the house. He had threatened to kill her on several occasions since she had left him. But what if Jamie really needed her? What if he was hurt? What if this was her last chance to get him off that property? Gail said a prayer that God would keep them all safe, and she promised herself that she would not pull onto the property. She would stop along the road on the berm. If Jamie came out by himself, she would wait for him. She was not sure what she would do if Ryan came along. All she knew was that one of her children needed her and she had to hurry.

It was nearly an hour's drive from her house to Ryan's. During that time she tried to concentrate on the highway and avoid hitting a deer. But in her mind many horrible possibilities chased each other around and around.

When she turned onto the lane where she had once lived, she could see her old house fully lit up. Every single light in the house seemed to be blazing. It was now after three in the morning. She could not help but wonder what would have made Ryan turn on all the lights. He was a frugal person who rarely allowed more than a single light to be turned on at a time. This was out of character. She pulled up to the edge of the driveway and turned around so she was headed back out. This also allowed her to be on the side nearest the house. She honked three times and waited. Jamie came running out carrying a paper bag, and far behind him came Ryan. She struggled to see whether Ryan carried a gun. It seemed as though his hands were empty, but she was still terrified. He could have a gun hidden in his waistband under his shirt.

Jamie tossed the bag onto the floor behind the passenger seat and jumped into the car. Jamie's clothes spilled out of the bag. His face was white with fear, but he didn't say a word.

Ryan approached her side of the car but stopped when she shouted, "That's close enough." For a few seconds they stared at each other in the dark until finally she found the courage to say, "What have you done to him?"

Ryan shook his head. "Call me when you get home. I'll tell you then." With that he turned on his heel and headed back to the house.

The drive home was awkward because Jamie refused to talk. He sat stone still, staring out the window, but he made no sound at all.

At the house she settled the babies back in their beds, knowing that they would be cranky in the morning because of this disruption. She gathered blankets, sheets, and a pillow and made up the couch for Jamie. Nearly everything she asked was met with stony silence. Only once he had settled under the blankets did he talk to her. "I'm safe here, right, Mom? You will call Dad?"

The sound of his voice took her back to when he was a little boy and the bad things had begun to bother him. She sat on the edge of the coffee table before the couch and took Jamie's hand in her own hand. "What happened tonight, honey?" she whispered.

Jamie shook his head and said, "I can't talk about it until tomorrow, Mom."

Gail went back to her bedroom and dialed the number for her old home. Ryan must've been waiting for the call, because he snatched the phone up on the first ring. "Now tell me what happened," Gail said by way of greeting.

Ryan began to cry. "You know I used to not believe you about that shadow man thing. I thought you were making it up to get attention. Then I saw stuff but I was always able to tell myself that it was an optical illusion or that I had imagined it. What happened here tonight, I did not imagine! My God, Gail, that thing is after Jamie."

Ryan continued to pour out his story. He said that he and Jamie had been fighting all evening. They fought about everything from the light bill to how much food Jamie was eating. Finally, around midnight, Jamie slammed out of the kitchen to go to the bathroom. Ryan was standing at the kitchen counter and watched the boy go down the hall. Ryan told Gail that he saw Jamie and Jamie's shadow going down the hall, but then a second, darker shadow peeled out of the wall and walked down the center of the hall behind Jamie. It followed him into the bathroom, and at that point Ryan found the strength to move. He ran down the hall and grabbed Jamie and told him what he had seen. Jamie did not seem a bit surprised. Jamie said that he knew that thing always got stronger when they were fighting. The shadow had been after him all his life, and it had only gotten worse since his mother had left. He told his father that the shadow would walk around and around his bed, touching him and poking at him throughout the night. Jamie often piled blankets and pillows over his head and body just so that he could rest.

Ryan then insisted that Jamie spend the night in the master bedroom with him. The two guys settled down on the king-size bed, and just as Ryan was about to go to sleep he heard Jamie gasp. Ryan opened his eyes to see the shadow figure standing directly beside Jamie. It was looking down at the two of them as though puzzled by what was going on. The figure reached out to touch Jamie, and instinctively Ryan swatted at it. His hand went through the blackness; he felt nothing. After that it was as though the shadow figure grew angry and decided to terrorize them. It walked through the room making sounds and paced around and around the bed. Ryan could barely believe what he was seeing. The shadow figure literally walked into the wall and out the other side as it circled the bed. It was then that Ryan had called for Gail to come and get Jamie. Whatever the shadow figure was, it seemed determined to terrify them that night.

Later Gail would speak with Jamie, and he told her that as he had grown older the shadow figure had gotten bolder with him. It touched him nearly every single night of his life. It circled his bed and made pounding noises in his room. It would scratch in his closet and shake his bed. He thought that it ate his fear to get strong.

Jamie spent the rest of his childhood living with his mother or his grandmother. He would struggle for most of his life to cope with the trauma of his childhood. He was damaged not only by the abuse from his father, but also by the shadow figure that had haunted him. As long as Jamie stayed away from his family's farm the shadow figure did not bother him, but when he would return there to visit his grandparents or to see his father for a few days, he could see or feel the presence of the shadow still watching him. He would never know exactly who or what the entity was, but he knew that it was dark and evil and that it wanted to see him hurt. He and his family firmly believe that this entity drew its power from fear, hate, and pain.

23

BEAUTY'S CURSE

Some twenty years after the American Civil War, the world was given a beautiful Christmas gift.

On Christmas Day 1884, in Tarentum, Pennsylvania, northeast of Pittsburgh on the Allegheny River, Florence Evelyn Nesbit was born. Neighbors from miles around would come to the Nesbit house just to gaze upon the most beautiful child they had ever seen.

As she grew toward her teenage years, she engaged in the typical pursuits of other young girls of the area and the era: Sunday school, summer picnics, sledding and ice-skating in the winter months. She even went to see the Pittsburgh Pirates play with her father. According to one biographer, she adored her father and lived for his praise.

And her father apparently returned her affection. He accumulated a library in their home of her favorite books and encouraged her to read. She was by nature outgoing and engaged in activities she thought might please him, like taking dance lessons, singing in the choir, and playing the piano. Due to a change in employment, her father, a lawyer, moved the family to Pittsburgh. Then Florence Evelyn's world caved in.

When she was eleven her father died suddenly at only forty years old. Since he was the main breadwinner in the family, Florence Evelyn, her younger brother, and her mother were left destitute. Within a month their house was foreclosed upon and their belongings auctioned, including all of Florence Evelyn's beloved books given to her by her father.

The family moved in with relatives and Mrs. Nesbit tried to find work as a seamstress. Debt mounted. The sense of security the family once knew had evaporated. The financial chaos spilled over into her family, and Florence Evelyn's normal childhood was interrupted. At first her mother mourned to extremes with fits of uncontrollable crying and grieving. Florence Evelyn and her brother slept with pillows over their heads to drown out their mother's agonized sobs.

Then one day Mrs. Nesbit's demeanor changed. She somehow drew herself up, pulled herself together, and began to move forward, going so far as to pack away all of her dead husband's portraits. Florence Evelyn would use this ability to turn off emotions herself one day soon.

Still, things got worse, if that was possible, and Mrs. Nesbit borrowed money and tried to make a living to sustain the family. She rented out rooms to male boarders but couldn't collect the often overdue rent herself. Instead she sent her budding daughter to talk to the men and collect the money. According to Florence Evelyn in later years, the experience was never pleasant. One can only imagine what the beautiful twelve-year-old was forced to observe while the boarders fumbled for the rent money.

Things continued to degrade. They were down to one meal a day when Florence Evelyn was sitting on their porch one sultry Sunday in August 1897 and a man with a camera happened to walk by. On a whim she approached him and asked if he would take her picture. The man just happened to be a professional photographer and was struck by the preteen's remarkable beauty, her piercing eyes and flowing abundance of hair. He took her picture but never got her name, and so the photo was published in a local paper without any documentation as to the lovely young girl's identity.

Their plague of poverty continued. It got so bad that one day Mrs. Nesbit screwed up her courage and approached one of Pittsburgh's wealthiest widowed philanthropists, Mrs. Mary Thaw, who lived in a magnificent mansion, named Lyndhurst. Mrs. Nesbit got no farther than the servant who answered the door and sent her away.

By 1898 Mrs. Nesbit, seeing no other option, moved to Philadelphia to seek work and left the children with family, then with friends. In Philadelphia she got a job at Wanamaker's and sent for the children. They, too, worked at the huge retail store. Still, there was never enough money.

One freezing day, Florence Evelyn was peering into a store window and a woman approached her and asked if she would like to pose for a portrait. Florence Evelyn said she would ask her mother, and when the two showed up at Mrs. Darach's studio, she posed for the portrait and earned one dollar for the five-hour session. Soon another artist asked her to pose. The two Nesbit women both suddenly realized that the daughter's delicate beauty might be a way out of poverty. Other artists began to admire her pure, childlike qualities offset by her luxurious dark hair, and she was introduced to an artists' colony, where her image was re-created in stained glass as the perfect form of an angel.

For young Florence Evelyn, it was fun because she could play dress-up as fairy tale characters: Bo Peep, a Gypsy girl, a nymph or milkmaid or goddess. The number of artists who wanted to capture her beauty grew. Soon, however, for the budding, vivacious teenager, sitting for hours in a smelly artists' loft grew wearisome. Thinking the medium would consist of her staying in one position for only a few minutes, she began posing for photographers.

Soon her image was peering out from posters, postcards, and advertisements. Writers in New York City began to mention her instead of the products she was advertising, and she became even more desired by women's magazines as the quintessential "American girl." It was not uncommon for her to show up in other notable publications of the new century. Charles Dana Gibson spotted her and used her in drawings of his "Gibson Girls," adding to her growing fame.

It was only a matter of time before she turned to the theater and, in spite of her young age, became a "Florodora Girl," dancing, singing, and acting on the New York stage. She also changed her name, dropping "Florence" and going with the name that became famous and synonymous with the epitome of twentieth-century American womanly beauty: Evelyn Nesbit.

As her face grew famous she began to leave a trail of besotted men, one of whom was himself quite famous. Architect Stanford White had designed the Vanderbilt Estate in Hyde Park, New York, as well as Madison Square Garden and many other buildings in New York

City. Though White was a known philanderer, scandalmongers went into overdrive when whispers began around the city that the married forty-eight-year-old was having an affair with teenaged Evelyn.

It was called "the Gilded Age," in no small part because of White's brash, over-the-top architectural designs, so you can imagine what his own New York City apartment looked like: huge ornate beds, garish artwork, opulent antique furniture, carved ceilings imported from Europe, plush red carpets, and rich ancient tapestries accentuated to an almost obscene level with the addition of a red velvet swing hanging from the ceiling.

Their relationship, at first, was platonic. Mrs. Nesbit had to return to Philadelphia several times and felt comfortable leaving her child in the care of "Stanny" White. Evelyn seemed to be merely arm candy for the wealthy, creative, popular architect. While Mrs. Nesbit sought a babysitter, perhaps Evelyn was seeking the fatherly relationship that had been cut short when she was eleven. But soon White's nefarious motive was revealed. Too many champagnes (and perhaps something slipped into the last one), and the next morning she woke in bed— next to White, a man old enough to be her father—a changed woman.

Evelyn, for reasons known only to the teenager, continued to see Stanny. In fact, between the champagne lunches and caviar and oyster dinners, their intimate life, which was orchestrated by one of the more creative minds of the Gilded Age, seemed to please the young girl from Tarentum. In her memoirs she spoke of being posed in positions like the artwork White had seen in his trips to the Louvre and other major galleries around Europe. He sometimes would hoist the diminutive Evelyn upon his shoulders and march her around his ornate bedroom. And then there was that velvet swing. . . .

But like many affairs, it burned hotly then settled down to a smolder. When White went off for his annual two-week hunting vacation, he left Evelyn in New York alone. It wasn't long before her lovely, youthful face caught the attention of another young, soon-to-be-famous face.

John (then called "Jack") Barrymore was the twenty-one-year-old sibling of Lionel and Ethel Barrymore, then king and queen of the

American theater. He was working as an illustrator in New York and had seen Evelyn in her current theater production—a dozen times. It just so happened that Evelyn, recently turned seventeen, had found Stanny's black book and realized that perhaps hers was not the only young torso that had been propelled on that red velvet swing. Jack and Evelyn soon began to be seen about town together, especially in the famous Algonquin Hotel restaurant.

It was a short but torrid romance, with Barrymore insisting his intentions were honorable—he wanted to marry Evelyn. But both her mother and Stanford White, who had come home to confront the couple as a sort of father figure, were against the union, mainly because Jack Barrymore was seen as a good-for-nothing loser. White then arranged for Evelyn to go to a private school in New Jersey.

Little did any of them know that a man—one of the richest in America—was watching them from a distance.

Harry K. Thaw, heir to the Thaw railroad fortune in Pittsburgh and son of none other than Mrs. Mary Thaw, denizen of Lyndhurst, where Evelyn's destitute mother was once turned away, had become enamored after also seeing Evelyn in a play—some forty times.

Perhaps *enamored* is not the right word. Because of his unstable personality, soon to have devastating consequences, perhaps *obsessed*, definitely *manipulative*, even *sociopathic* might be better terms to describe the spoiled child of the Gilded Age.

He managed to wrangle an introduction to Evelyn but used an assumed name; he dropped to his knees upon meeting her and kissed the hem of her dress. During one of their conversations, Thaw offered that she should keep away from Stanford White, a married man with a horrid reputation. She refused to tell him where she and her mother were staying in New York. It didn't matter, for he already knew, having employed his own spies from the Pinkerton Detective Agency.

Thaw finally ended his charade and confessed to being the son of one of the richest families in America, but at the time Evelyn was still not impressed. Having grown up in Pittsburgh (albeit on the other side of the tracks), she had heard, like everyone else, of the Thaws. What she had not heard about, mainly because of his overseeing mother, was Harry Thaw's dark side. Never having had to grow up because of his parents' wealth, he still retained some of the affectations of childhood: giggling childishly at the misfortunes of others, throwing expensive plates at the heads of servants who displeased him, and talking in baby talk.

It got worse. He was also known for engaging prostitutes who left his apartment with welts, bruises, and tales of handcuffs, ropes, and riding crops. Yet, in spite of his own sordid proclivities, he had a sort of "virgin obsession."

Evelyn endured his avalanche of phone calls, mash notes, and tokens of endearment, and after a month began (somehow) to feel affection toward the spoiled man-boy, forming what she saw as a "genial friendship." Surprisingly (or not so, if you consider his manipulative character), he agreed that boarding school was the place for her, not the seedy theater life. And before she left for school, he proposed marriage.

She turned him down, probably (according to Paula Uruburu in her biography of Nesbit) because Evelyn knew of his obsession with purity and, after her dalliances with Stanford White, she could not be hypocritical. She, of course, knew nothing yet of Thaw's bizarre bedroom rituals.

But he already knew, through his network of spies, all about her and Stanny's.

While in school, in April 1903 Evelyn suffered an attack of appendicitis and was operated on by a surgeon supplied by Harry Thaw, who suggested that a trip to Europe would help her recovery.

It all seemed perfectly safe to begin with: Mrs. Nesbit and Evelyn would sail on a liner and Harry would follow two days later. They would first meet in London, then go to Paris. Of course they would have separate rooms, if not hotels, wherever they went. Harry, however, had created a micro-itinerary that would drive anyone mad. Horseraces, parties, posh suppers, shopping trips, visits to the Louvre, drives through the countryside, all orchestrated to exhaust Mrs. Nesbit, the chaperone. It worked, and she returned to London and eventually to the United States.

All this time Harry continued to press eighteen-year-old Evelyn for her hand in marriage. One night, after a refusal, he demanded to know the truth as to why she would not marry him. Perhaps hoping that the truth about her relationship with White would drive him away, she began a confession, to which Harry played "good cop."

As her sordid tale of her affair with White slowly emerged, Harry theatrically rose from his chair and flung himself down, sobbing, "Poor child!" His moans filled the room for two hours as he encouraged her to tell every slimy detail. He tore at his hair, chewed his bottom lip, and whimpered pitifully . . . but continued to egg her on. He blamed Mrs. Nesbit for allowing her daughter into the clutches of such a fiend. But most of all he blamed his ultimate, inexorable nemesis, Stanford White.

They left Paris on a whirlwind tour of Europe: Holland, Munich, Innsbruck, and Tyrol, where Harry had rented an entire castle for three weeks. Seemingly a fairy tale setting, for Evelyn it soon became a house of horrors.

For two days Harry bossed the staff around, finally dismissing them. After dinner one evening, Evelyn was exhausted and wished to sleep. Harry kissed her demurely on the forehead, and she went to her own room to fall asleep immediately. She hardly realized she was now alone in this ancient edifice with a monster.

Fifteen minutes later she was awakened by an unclad Harry tearing off her nightgown, swinging a riding crop, and howling about sin, immorality, and wicked behavior like the madman he was. The assault went on and on, Evelyn wondering, so close to her surgery, if she would even survive. Harry became incoherent during the rape, prattling about chastity, debauchery, innocence lost. When he was finished, he began, like a medieval inquisitor, to query again about her relationship with White.

The next day, with Evelyn hiding her bruises, Harry acted as if nothing had happened. They continued their grand tour. But back in Paris, Evelyn confided in two friends visiting from New York as to Thaw's vicious, perverted attack. They secured passage for her back to the United States. Harry paid for it, never acknowledging that his actions were the cause.

Once she was back in New York, Stanford White visited her. Immediately, he tried to kiss her, but she pushed him away. He sat and began to tell her—obviously a little too late—about the real Harry Thaw. He announced that Thaw was a drug addict, which may have contributed to his maniacal attack. White ordered her not to see him again.

Still shy of nineteen years old, Evelyn had been through a lifetime of experience—some of it good, much of it frightening, some of it even horrifying, all of it brought on by her gift of physical beauty. Had she blossomed into a classic beauty just a few years later, perhaps she would have had the maturity to see through the intricate machinations of the two obsessive master manipulators who pursued her. The strange part is, they both warned her sincerely and truthfully about the other, yet her youth and naiveté refused to allow her to believe either one. So her magnificent beauty continued to take her down.

With the help of a nefarious lawyer, White had her detail (in the lawyer's words) an affidavit telling all about Thaw's behavior in Europe. He also had friends contact her with the worst tales about Thaw they could conjure: dope fiend, rapist, sadist, and so forth.

Thaw's detectives also tracked her down, and she had a meeting with him and his own lawyer. He, of course, denied everything and attributed all the stories to attempts at blackmailing a very rich man (him). Somehow Evelyn believed him and actually thought it was she who had wronged him!

As she went back to work on the stage, Harry began his siege: offering to pay her whatever she was making in the theater, tracking her down at dinner, denying his drug use, saying that he had been a victim of temporary insanity on their night in the castle. After weeks of this, Evelyn was weakening.

After another bout with appendicitis and a month's recuperation, as well, no doubt, as a continuous fusillade of proposals from Harry, she relented and married him on April 5, 1905.

The Thaws rubbed elbows with the Carnegies and Vanderbilts. Evelyn, beautiful as she was, to Mrs. Thaw was still just a showgirl. It mattered not to Harry, smitten to the core. He was somewhat handsome, young, wealthy beyond belief, and just smooth enough for the girl from Tarentum to accept as a husband.

Evelyn spent time at both Lyndhurst and Elmhurst, the family summer home near Cresson, Pennsylvania, expecting to play hostess to the panoply of early twentieth-century notables who visited the Thaws, such as Helen Keller, Thomas Edison, and writer Edward Stratemeyer. Instead she was snubbed by her in-laws while privately abused by her husband. The sadistic sexual torture grew in intensity, but the bruises and suffering were hidden from public view. Strangely, Harry became insanely jealous; if a man so much as spoke to Evelyn, she was accused of having an affair and punished for it. As well, his obsession with Stanford White grew even more intense. And, at odd moments, he forced her to repeat her confession of her acts with White.

Harry scheduled a trip to New York City. Privately Evelyn was elated. She had friends there, people she could talk to other than her obsessed husband. People who might even help her escape.

As soon as they arrived in New York she dispatched a letter to Stanford White, explaining the horror she found herself in and pleading for help. After a while Harry Thaw heard the rumors that his wife and her former paramour had resumed their affair, and Thaw forbade her to have any contact with White or even speak his name. One can only imagine what went through Thaw's strange mind. Obsessed with his wife—one of the most beautiful women on the planet and supposed willing accomplice to his every sexually sadistic whim— and yet seeing her run to the man who introduced her to sex via the red velvet swing and all.

One evening in June 1906, Harry and Evelyn attended an event at Madison Square Garden. Who should walk in but the designer of the magnificent New York landmark, Stanford White. Harry went over the edge, verbally abusing his wife in that public place and accusing her of carrying on her sordid affair with White right before his very eyes. Evelyn denied it all, refusing to even look in White's direction and periodically pleading with Harry to leave the Garden. Thaw refused and continued to seethe.

Intermission came. Thaw excused himself from his wife, walked over to White, and shot him with a pistol, once in the shoulder and twice in the back of the head, killing him instantly.

"I did it because he ruined my wife!" he cried. "He had it coming to him. He took advantage of the girl and then deserted her!"

Considering that White and Evelyn had begun their very public affair nearly five years before and that Harry Thaw knew all about it, his shouted confession rang hollow.

What ensued was "the Trial of the Century," which was easy to name since the century was still very new.

Almost immediately after his arrest, Thaw's lawyers hired "alienists," the predecessors of criminal psychiatrists, also known in those days as "bug doctors." He was charged with homicide in the first degree, meaning the murder was willfully committed. The defense, over the Thaw family's objections, would try to argue temporary insanity. As the trial progressed, details of it were a daily staple of newspapers across the country.

Evelyn had to testify. Worse, as part of the defense strategy, she had to relate what she had told Harry in Paris about all the things she and Stanford White had done. The prosecuting attorney (known as "the Tiger") dove in and tried to break her down. Evelyn, the beautiful girl from Tarentum, after all the cross-examinations from Harry Thaw, fended off the Tiger with skill and drew the admiration and sympathy of the press. Some days, when she exited the courthouse, she was mobbed with women just wanting to touch her dress or hoping she would glance their way. Hundreds of thousands of postcards featuring her face and figure were sold in a month.

The trial lasted two and a half months and ended in a hung jury.

The second trial went more quickly, mainly because the Thaws did not argue strategy; they saw that the only way to save Harry from the electric chair was the temporary insanity defense. Evelyn again had to recite the sordid details of her private life with Harry and Stanny, and, in spite of others who had occupied the position, she became known forever as "the Girl in the Red Velvet Swing."

Though Harry was acquitted and committed to an asylum for the criminally insane, his loving mother spent vast sums of money to keep him comfortable in a private room with catered meals. There was no such love for Evelyn: She had debased herself twice in a public court to save Harry, but the Thaws still cut her off monetarily.

Once again, Evelyn was on her own.

Harry and Evelyn continued to see each other while he was incarcerated. That is, until he couldn't get his way by proving himself miraculously cured of his insanity right away. As his incarceration extended over the years, the relationship soured, then turned ugly, but not until after Evelyn found herself pregnant. He denied that the child was his. They finally divorced in 1915.

She got back into show business for a while, married her dance partner, and then got divorced, never to marry again. The Roaring Twenties were not kind to her. Nor was the rest of her life, marked by drug and alcohol abuse, suicide attempts, barroom brawls, failed businesses, unpaid bills, and sales of her belongings (except for her pet boa constrictor, which escaped into Greenwich Village before it could be sold). A 1955 movie called *The Girl in the Red Velvet Swing* (of course) was made about her early life, forever sealing her public image.

Her one lasting legacy was her son, Russell, who became a storied test pilot, air racer, and, according to some sources, World War II ace. Evelyn eventually moved to California and taught sculpting. She died in a nursing home in 1967.

Apparently, even the grave brought no peace to Evelyn.

In 1968 a young couple with small children moved into a trailer on the 255-acre Elmhurst estate, contracted by the Westminster Presbytery of Pittsburgh to care for the property and cook and clean for groups using the twenty-one-room Tudor-style mansion for retreats. Odd happenings began their first few weeks there.

Bodiless footsteps paced the hallway of the trailer, the thermostat kept dialing itself back at night, and pounding at the back door kept the couple awake at night, though no one was found outside the door. A male voice called out the woman's name when no one else was home.

In the mansion they were often alone, preparing for the next retreat. Voices were heard in the bedroom above the dining room, angry voices, fighting. They couldn't make out what was being said; all they could tell was that it was a man and a woman. Commonplace items were removed for a while, then returned to their place by unseen hands; the woman was often touched in the kitchen while she worked. She reported having her hair twirled playfully and the invasive feeling of being petted.

When their friends visited the mansion, it was reported that they saw a beautiful young woman in a turn-of-the-century hat and gown standing on the stairs to the first floor. Even retreat guests reluctantly confessed to seeing the young woman and hearing footsteps and the voices.

Eventually the church removed the trailer from the property and the family moved into the house, occupying the third floor. A couple stopped in to visit one day and informed them that they had been caretakers of the mansion years before. When asked if anything strange had occurred to them during their tenure, the older caretakers described some ghostly activity. They had never seen the beautiful young woman, but they had resided there before Evelyn died in 1967.

While, for the most part, the family never felt afraid of the presences in the mansion, one day that changed. The woman was escorting a young lady on a tour of Elmhurst for a paper she was writing. As she took the girl through, she felt a gradually escalating sense of dread. By the time they reached the second floor, she was almost overwhelmed by an urge to get out of the house. She finally confessed to the young woman her fear, and the young woman agreed: She, too, had felt a mounting horror. Once outside, the girl paused to take a photo of the empty mansion. There, in a second-floor window, was a face scowling at them.

A reporter for the nearby Johnstown newspaper wrote a story on the haunting at Elmhurst. Later she returned with some friends to spend the night. What started out as a fun-filled evening of ghost stories ended up a restless night vainly searching for sleep. In the morning one of the reporter's friends told of something icy cold and yet invisible caressing her lips.

Today Elmhurst is a private home, and no further stories of supernatural happenings have emerged from it. But according to one psychic who toured the property, there are seven spirits there. One is a pretty young woman with abundant dark hair; another is a slim young man with slicked-back dark hair. There is also a darker entity that may have been responsible for knocking over the chair of one of the residents' daughters several times.

As to the identity of the mischievous wraiths, one can only speculate. But it cannot be too far a leap to imagine Harry, his mother, and Evelyn having returned in spirit form, to rehash the troubles they once had while earthbound.

24

THE HAUNTING
OF AL CAPONE

On February 14, 1929, the holiday dedicated to love changed forever. In the garage of SMC Cartage, 2122 North Clark Street in the Lincoln Park section of Chicago's North Side, a large dog was barking and howling uncontrollably. Mrs. Landesman, who operated a boarding-house across the street, sent one of her tenants over to the garage to see what was upsetting the dog. The tenant saw the dog tied to the bumper of a car, and beyond the animal she saw a sight that drove her from the garage.

The floor of the garage and the back wall were a bloody mess. Seven well-dressed men were sprawled in front of the wall, contorted by death. They were perforated by .45 caliber bullets. Shotgun blasts had nearly obliterated the faces of two. Incredibly, one of the men still moved.

The police were called. Bystanders were confused. Not long before they had seen two policemen and two civilians enter the building. In a few minutes the officers led the two civilians out of the garage, apparently under arrest. They entered a car and drove off.

It was a ruse. The "police" were hit men in police uniforms. The four men were later identified as gang members from the South Side Italian gang sent to murder George "Bugs" Moran, leader of the North Side's Irish gang.

The only problem was, "Bugs" was not in the crowd gunned down that St. Valentine's Day.

Regardless, the "police" and civilian hit men lined up the seven facing the wall and emptied seventy rounds into them, continuing to fire even after they hit the floor. To make sure they were dead, a shotgun was used on two. Frank Gusenberg, a member of the Moran gang, survived long enough to be taken to the hospital with fourteen gunshot wounds. When police asked who shot him, he replied, "No one shot me." Even though his own brother was killed in the garage, at least he wasn't a snitch when he died a few hours later.

What does the crime that became known as the "St. Valentine's Day Massacre" in Chicago have to do with a curse in the Commonwealth of Pennsylvania?

The murders were part of the ongoing turf wars between Moran and the famous Chicago gangster Al Capone. For years things had been heating up between the North Siders and South Siders over retaliation killings, Moran's takeover of some Capone saloons he claimed were in his territory, and a dispute over Capone's dog race-track business just outside Chicago. Underlying it all was a fight over the bootlegging of whiskey, the most lucrative of black market businesses during Prohibition.

In an era that was filled with colorful characters, Capone was perhaps the most famous. It was a time when being a bank robber not only brought you wealth and fame, but could also get you gunned down on sight by police. It ushered in the naming of "Public Enemy Number 1," and the incursion of the federal government to help local law enforcement capture criminals who, because of the automobile, were highly mobile and crisscrossed states lines to do their crimes.

Capone was in just that situation when he traveled to Philadelphia shortly after the St. Valentine's Day Massacre and was caught with a concealed weapon. For this he bought time in Pennsylvania's notorious Eastern State Penitentiary.

The prison was conceived of in 1787 by a group of men influenced by the Quaker tenet of repentance being the road to salvation; they met in none other than Benjamin Franklin's home in Philadelphia. Granted, the penal system in America was abhorrent, based more on punishment than reeducation toward the correct societal behavior. The Pennsylvania Quakers intended to change that.

Their new gaol would be called a "penitentiary," a quiet place of solitude where inmates could become penitent, reflect inwardly on their sins, and repent to their god. With souls scrubbed clean, they would be released back into society as good, productive citizens. It was to be a gentle reconditioning. But it became a new brand of hell on earth.

When it opened in 1829, the thoroughly modern design was supposed to facilitate both the jobs of the guards and the mental reflections of the incarcerated, thought to be so essential for rehabilitation. Architect John Haviland originally designed the facility to house 250 "penitents." He sadly underestimated the number of Pennsylvania miscreants; before long he was forced to modify the structure to contain 450. To help the guards with their jobs, the original design was in the shape of a wagon wheel, with the guard station in the middle "hub" so they could watch all the cell corridors at a glance.

Eastern State Penitentiary was the first public building in America to have running water and indoor plumbing in each cell. Being the first to have indoor plumbing, it was also a test case. Unfortunately, the sewer pipes ran alongside the water pipes. When the boilers heated the water, the sewage warmed up as well, filling the building with an unbreathable stench.

The individual cells were also unique. The doors were extremely short, so to enter their cells, the prisoners had to bow, reminding them to remain humble. Each cell was lit by a single, small skylight known as "the Eye of God," forcing prisoners to glance heavenward to remind them of the all-seeing, all-knowing deity.

From the beginning the doctrine of shameful introspection was enforced: New prisoners were examined and details were recorded; their civilian clothes were taken from them and they were given a uniform with numbers sewn on it; before being led to their cell, a black hood was placed over their heads and the isolation began.

They would not see or hear another inmate since they were kept in their own cells until their sentence was fulfilled. They couldn't talk, sing, tap their feet or hands, or convey any sound. Guards who came to inspect them wore socks over their shoes so as to make the silence complete. The prisoners were allowed no outside contact with friends or family. They could have but one book in their cells: the Bible. All their time was to be spent reflecting upon their misdeeds, and, perhaps on more than one occasion, their slowly approaching insanity.

Should prisoners break any of the harsh rules, they were stripped naked in their cells. Blankets were taken and they were left, even in winter, to endure the exposure. No doubt they were reminded how much like a tomb the cells appeared.

For the worst offenders the guards came up with the "ice bath," tossing ice water on the stripped inmates. In the winter this was done outside and the water froze on the skin. This was repeated, over and over.

There was the "mad chair," where an inmate would be strapped tightly without food or water, sometimes for days. Limbs would atrophy and turn black from lack of circulation. The name of the chair apparently came from the mental state of those subjected to the punishment.

For those who broke the silence rule, there was the "iron gag," a metal device clamped on the tongue and attached to the wrists, which were chained behind the inmate's back. Any movement at all sliced the tongue.

While the Quakers were not in charge of the daily administration of Eastern State Penitentiary, it was their philosophy that led to the isolation of prisoners, a practice used to this day. The real effects of solitary confinement upon prisoners are just now being understood.

Modern prisoners in isolation find themselves talking out loud, singing—anything to hear another human voice. This, of course, was disallowed at Eastern State, unless you wanted to wear the iron gag.

Inmates in isolation experience feelings of total worthlessness and deep depression, wondering if their guard is ever going to return to check on them. According to university studies, after being in isolation for just three months, prisoners universally display anxiety and paranoia, begin to compulsively clean or exercise, and have problems with memory and concentration. They demonstrate sleeping disorders and have more headaches than normal as well as a high suicide rate.

Those who have been in isolation for years withdraw into themselves, not knowing what will bring on another session of isolation. Even after they are released into society, they gradually continue their withdrawal, are angry for no reason, have imaginary ailments such as itches and growths on the body that aren't really there, and begin patterns of self-harm (such as cutting or mutilating themselves) as evidence to themselves of their freedom. Often they will do this to feel the touch of others: the doctors or nurses that must now care for them.

All this, of course, was unknown when Al Capone served his time.

Eastern State Penitentiary was one hundred years old when Capone served his eight months. Things had changed at Eastern State, especially for Capone, since the Quakers first planned the repentance-based incarceration. It was Capone's first time in jail, and he made the best of it. Instead of the cold stone walls and unfurnished space that surrounded other prisoners, Capone had a carpet, a desk, a wingback chair, a cabinet radio, fancy electric lamps, potted plants, and artwork. It was more appropriate for a business-man's office than a jail cell, and he met with his lawyers and other business associates there. Though he denied any complicity in the St. Valentine's Day Massacre, one of the victims may have had a hand in Capone's "confession."

On their late-night rounds the guards would hear talking and moaning coming from Capone's cell. Moving closer, they would hear him talking to "Jimmy," pleading for him to leave him alone. Guards would peer into the cell and see Capone by himself. Later they found out that Capone believed he was being haunted by the spirit of Albert Kachellek, aka James Clark, Bugs Moran's second-in-command.

That ghost seems to have been attached more to Al Capone than to Eastern State since, when the gangster was serving time for income tax evasion on Alcatraz Island, James Clark apparently followed him. The guards there also heard him begging Clark to leave him alone.

Some would like to chalk this up to the dementia Capone was suffering from due to an untreated case of syphilis, but Hymie Cornish, Capone's valet, claimed to have seen Clark's spirit. Even while Capone was staying in his lush apartment in Chicago, Capone's bodyguards broke into the suite after hearing their boss wailing for Jimmy to leave him alone. They found no one there but Capone, disturbed because Jimmy had visited him again.

But even without the spirit of James Clark, Eastern State Penitentiary has its fair share of restless specters roaming the crusty hallways and inhabiting the abandoned cells.

Since 1971 the facility has been designated a national historic landmark. It was sold to the city of Philadelphia, and the Pennsylvania Prison Society of Philadelphia now administrates it. Various fundraisers are held each year, including tours, masquerades, and even a prison food tasting. But ghost aficionados have been collecting tales of the unexplained that have surfaced in the years since it was closed as an active prison.

Many people have reported seeing black shadows slinking through the long-abandoned areas of the penitentiary. Could these be the types of ghosts known as "shadow people"? Although most people think that ghosts appear only as white, mist-like apparitions, there is also a supernatural phenomenon that appears black, often wearing a long dark coat and some kind of a hat. Could this be what some have seen roaming the halls?

As well, visitors have heard talking and laughing, footsteps, and even screams emanating from the deserted cells.

Cellblock 12 has echoed with eerie laughter. When investigated, the cells are as empty as they have been for decades. Cellblock 6 is where the shadow people are often seen lurking. Visitors have seen individuals enter cells, but when they are followed into the cell, the room is empty. Death Row is also haunted by those mysterious shadow people; one was seen running down the hall, ducking into and out of the cells.

If you don't believe it, plan a visit. Walking to the infirmary, you will hear whispering coming from the cells you pass, although no human being is there to make the noise. Once in the infirmary you will feel nervous, as if you are being watched. Perhaps you will hear what paranormal investigation groups have recorded there: voices where there is no human to create the sound. You may glance up to see a guard in the central guard tower, still adhering to his sworn duty, keeping vigil on inmates as dead as he is.

Or you may be as unlucky as a locksmith was once. Called in to work on some rusty locks, he was bothered by the intense feeling of being watched. Try as he might to see if any of the staff had entered his work space, he saw no one. Concentrating more on his work did no good. Unconsciously his eyes were drawn from the lock to catch the person watching him, to no avail. Finally, nearly finished with his work, he glanced behind him just in time to see a dark figure lunge across the hall at him. He rapidly finished up and exited the prison.

With the historic documentation of human suffering within the walls of Eastern State, it is no wonder that overnight visitors (yes, you can sign up to sleep there!) have reported that they are convinced that some perturbed spirits remain. Some remain to fulfill a duty to guard, some perhaps because they remain guarded by other spirits. You've heard the expression that the inmates are running the asylum? At Eastern State it seems that the inmates are running the penitentiary long after they completed their sentences here on earth.

25

LITTLE RED MUSTANG

It stood there red and shiny, and Terry could not help but smile. The little cherry-red 1968 Mustang was beautiful but totally impractical. Terry had five children and needed a car for work, but he could not help himself. He wanted that car. The price was more than reasonable, and he had checked the engine out himself. The engine was sound. The body was amazingly good for a vehicle that old. Terry knew that he should not buy it, but he also knew that he was going to.

The little coupe came home with Terry, and for the first few weeks the car made the rounds of family members as Terry showed it off. His family was filled with car enthusiasts, and everyone duly admired the car as Terry drove them around and showed them how it handled.

The family smiled indulgently and allowed Terry his pleasure. Terry had seen more than his share of troubles and responsibilities through the years. His family was happy to see that the car was giving him such joy. They refrained from pointing out that it was not the best choice for the long drive back and forth to work over the mountains daily. They did not mention that it did not easily accommodate his five children, or the fact that it did not have the best gas mileage. They simply shook their heads quietly and agreed with him that the car was great.

It was great, at least for the first few weeks. Every morning Terry got in and headed up Route 22 over Short Mountain to work. The car took the journey easily. He sipped his coffee and tooled along, feeling young and carefree in the coupe.

But then one day he saw the temporary road sign warning that soon the route to Short Mountain was going to be shut down for road construction. Terry realized that he'd have to take the detour up through Frankstown and around Duncansville into Altoona on Route 764. It was longer, but there really was nothing that he could do about it.

Perhaps no one in the family loved the Mustang more than Terry's fifteen-year-old sister. The car had rolled off the assembly line the same year that she had been born, and she desperately wanted the vehicle if and when Terry ever got rid of it. He would laugh when she pleaded with him, and eventually he made her the promise that when he was done with the car she could have it.

On the first day that the detour was to take effect, Terry left for work a little early. He knew that the detour would take longer to complete. The car drove as beautifully as ever. The steering was smooth and responsive to his every touch. Terry followed the road up along the edge of Frankstown. There the road literally ran through a cemetery. Crews had cut the cemetery on the hill in half to put the road in. A retaining wall had been built along the upper part of the road to keep the cemetery from sliding down over the highway or washing out.

Terry slowed the car slightly as he entered the cemetery area. Suddenly the car seemed to slide, as if it had hit ice or an oil slick. Terry felt the steering wheel jerking from side to side in his hands. He struggled to gain control as the back end fishtailed and the car slewed around. Suddenly the retaining wall was directly in front of him. Terry fought the wheel, but it was as if something was turning the wheel toward the wall. He white-knuckled the wheel and gave it a great turn to the left. The car shot out of the area of the cemetery and Terry immediately gained control again. He twisted the wheel back and forth slightly, testing how much control he had as he eased off the road onto a wide spot. His heart was beating rapidly. He had nearly hit the retaining wall.

Terry tried to calm his breathing and his mind. He forced himself to accept that he had hit something slick, but in the back of his mind there was a prickle of doubt. He had been driving a long time, and he knew that what had happened was not an ordinary skid. It had felt as if he was wrestling someone for the steering wheel. As if someone had tried to make him hit the wall, but that was crazy and impossible.

He pushed the idea away and eased the vehicle onto the road. Now the steering wheel played smoothly in his hands again. He tensed, but the steering gave him no further problems.

Terry took the same route home again, but the car worked fine. He wanted to believe that the morning incident was just a fluke, and he felt almost foolish after passing through the cemetery again.

That night he told his brother, Jerry, about the morning events at the cemetery. Jerry was a mechanic and he listened to Terry's story carefully. "Let's take her for a ride," he muttered and got in the driver's seat. He'd check it out for himself.

The ride went smoothly and Jerry could not find a thing wrong with the steering. "You must have hit ice," he told Terry laughingly. "There's nothing wrong with this steering. Little brother, you are crazy."

The next morning Terry slowed down as he approached the cemetery road. He watched the road carefully and held on to the steering wheel tightly. At first it all seemed just fine, but then he felt a sudden hitch in the steering. The wheel jerked right in his hands as if someone had grabbed it from him. He clutched at the wheel as a thread of fear shot through him. He had been watching the road; there had been no ice and no oil slick. Suddenly the wheel wrenched hard to the right and he felt himself losing control of the car. His heart slammed in his chest. The car was accelerating despite the fact that his foot was crushed down hard on the brake.

"No," he screamed, pulling the wheel left with all his might. "No!" The back of the car slid around and he struggled to gain control. The wall was suddenly before him, and then the car spun further and he barely missed the wall. He shot out the other side of the cemetery and pulled over in the same spot where he had the day before.

Shaking, he slammed the car into park and cut the engine. The car sat there ticking slightly as the engine began to cool. He grabbed a cigarette from the pack on the passenger's seat and rolled down the window. With shaking fingers he lit the cigarette and breathed in deeply. He shivered from cold and reaction. Something had happened back there, and it was not something that he could explain. He thought about getting out of the car, but somehow that didn't seem right. He was frightened, and in his mind he barely acknowledged that he feared the car would start by itself.

He checked his watch and realized that if he did not get moving, he'd be late for work. With the thought of his five children spurring him onward, he gingerly turned the ignition key. The car roared to life and he eased it back out onto the road. He drove slower than normal, but once again the car was responding to his every movement. Terry could not shake the feeling that someone else had been fighting him for the wheel of the car back in the cemetery. The idea was so insane that he knew he had to put it away. It was a problem with the steering, and that was all it was.

Terry held his breath when he drove back through the cemetery that night, but once again the steering was smooth and he passed through without trouble. Still, he had to get to the bottom of the problem, which meant that he had to deal with whatever was causing the steering issue. He simply was not going to think about anything else.

That night Terry insisted that Jerry help him as he went over the steering. Terry tore the whole mechanism apart. He and Jerry laid everything on a plastic tarp to put back in. They looked for patterns of wear or anything else that could be wrong. They found nothing.

Terry got Jerry to drive him to work for the next two days while the car was still in pieces, and on those days the trip through the cemetery went smoothly. Of course, the Mustang was sitting in Jerry's backyard, and Terry had to admit that he was glad he was not driving it.

Over the weekend Terry and Jerry finished reassembling the vehicle. They had gone over it in minute detail. He and Jerry took it for a ride and it worked just fine. Terry drove it along the road through the cemetery and it did not falter at all. Terry had been thinking crazy thoughts, but that drive allayed them and he knew that Monday morning he'd be fine.

Monday morning dawned gray and sullen. A cold wind blew and little ice particles slashed at Terry's face as he hurried toward the car. Inside he shivered and started the engine. He waited several minutes in the early morning cold for the car to warm up. Then he started out. He drove without incident until he saw the detour sign. At that moment a little thread of fear grabbed him, but he pushed it away. He needed to get to work and there was no time for foolishness.

Instinctively he slowed down as he started through the cemetery. He was nearly halfway through when he felt the wheel give a sharp twist. His hands tightened, but the wheel had been grabbed so roughly that it slid through his fingers. He slammed his foot on the brake while he wrestled for the wheel. He encountered something hard and unyielding beneath his grasp. It felt like fingers. He could not see them, but he could feel them. They gripped the wheel and jerked it, twisting the car toward the retaining wall. His heart leapt as the wall loomed, and he barely twisted the wheel enough to avoid a direct hit. He heard the metal grind against the wall as they connected.

Something or someone stomped on the gas, accelerating the car forward as the wheel tried to turn back toward the wall. Terry stomped the brake hard, but the car still accelerated. It shot forward and past the cemetery. Suddenly the car smoothed out and he felt the wheel respond to him again. He slammed on the brakes and brought the Mustang to an abrupt halt. He was shaking and sweating. He thought he'd pass out, but he didn't dare. If he lost control, the car might take off again. He slammed the car into park and pulled out the keys. Even then he wasn't sure it wouldn't start again on its own. The whole thing made no good sense, but some-thing—someone—had tried to kill him. Only when going through the cemetery . . . only in the mornings . . .

Terry took the car home that day and parked it. He managed to round up enough cash to buy an old clunker. He had to go back on his word to his sister. He couldn't give her the car, but he was cer-tainly done with it. He would never again drive that cursed Mustang. Someone or something bad was attached to that car. He knew that it sounded insane, but whatever it was had tried to kill him.

Terry had the car hauled to the junkyard. He insisted on watching as it was crushed because he feared that someone would try to restore the car. He could not let it take anyone's life.

26

THE CURSED TRAIN

Railroading lore is filled with stories of haunted trains and ghostly engineers who haunt the tracks where they died, but there are darker stories of hoodoo trains and cursed trains that carry a stigma with them. The little rusted narrow-gauge train that sat in a field between the towns of Schellsburg and Bedford seemed to be just a lost piece of history, until someone took the time to learn that it was a cursed train that had taken lives.

There are two different types of train tracks. The regular-gauge tracks are those that most people are familiar with, but there are narrow-gauge tracks, too. Those were often used by smaller railroads and businesses that used smaller trains. Nonetheless, these tracks were workhorses that bore wood, lumber, coal, and much more and were vital to a growing nation.

Engine 49 was a narrow-gauge engine put on line sometime in the 1940s. The exact date it began service is not known, but the date when the engine began evidencing its curse is well known.

In 1947 the engine was working at the Jamesville Quarry in New York with "side-dump" cars that would tip sideways to offload what they held. The engine was dumping quarry rock into a crusher. The engineer would have to back the train up, car by car, as each load was dumped into the crusher. The track was built out beside the crusher and went back far enough for the engineer to empty a specific number of cars by slowly reversing and backing up each car. The track just dropped off at the far end, and so it was vital that the engineer pay close attention to what he was doing.

It was around eight o'clock at night when the engineer was off-loading into the crusher. It was slow, boring work, and the engineer found himself nodding off as he eased the train back car by car.

Suddenly the engineer startled awake as the train seemed to be pulled backward off the track. He reacted instinctively and jumped for the side of the hill the trestle ran beside. He landed with a jolt as the train fell off the end of the track and right into the crusher building. There was screaming and a terrible crash that echoed through the small valley. There was a wall of steam coming up, and then flames erupted.

Two men were killed and others injured when the train crashed into the fifth floor of the crushing building. Fortunately, the death toll was slim because the framing held and the train did not go into the floors below.

Engine 49 was removed in pieces and sent to a company called Alco to be repaired. The train accident had cost over one hundred thousand dollars.

Alco completely reconstructed the train. Because the boiler and water tank were compromised by the crash, they were removed and new ones were installed. Everyone working on the rails knew that the most important things an engine had were the water tank and boiler. They were vital to move the train, and they were deadly if not maintained properly.

In 1950 engine 49 was put back to work in the quarry. It did not take long for the train to find trouble. It had been working only a few weeks when one night, around eight o'clock, the train was sitting on the track waiting its turn to dump. The engineer had the steam up so that the train was ready to move when it got its turn. Suddenly the new steam line broke loose, hitting the engineer and killing him instantly.

The train was quickly removed from service. The train crews and the quarry men alike did not want to work around engine 49. People began calling it "the Ghost." It had claimed three men's lives in as many years.

However, businesses are not sentimental about their equipment. Engine 49 was valuable, and a great deal of money had been spent on repairing it. The train was gone over once more and then put back into service.

The word spread quickly among the engineers that engine 49 was cursed. Those brave enough to work the engine reported that at eight o'clock the smell of burning flesh filled the little engine and forced them out. No one wanted to be aboard the train—particularly at that time of night.

The quarrymen also feared the engine. Had not the first two victims been workers at the quarry? They talked about how the train's bell would ring when no one was in the train and how the whistle would blow despite the fact that no one was physically in the engine to pull the whistle chain. Most of what happened occurred to the evening crew, and it usually happened around eight o'clock.

Finally things reached a point where the engineers refused to work on engine 49. The Jamesville Quarry might have put money into the train, but the men refused to risk their lives.

The question of retiring engine 49 became moot when the quarry shut down in 1953. The engine sat for approximately a year, and then it was put up for sale along with other trains and railroad items. Engine 49 was purchased by Rail City, a New York museum that celebrated the railroad industry, at an auction. Engine 49 seemed content to sit there in the yard of Rail City and be part of the display. No one fired up the engine, and it seemed safe enough. The administration had heard whispers that the train was cursed, that it was a death train, but that was foolishness.

From 1954 until the mid-1970s, the train sat quietly without fire in its belly or steam in its lines. The museum staff decided that the accidents and the nickname "the Ghost" were great marketing tools, so they told the story for the tourists. But no one really believed a word of the silly legend. Cursed trains that took lives were just the imaginings of superstitious people.

In the mid-1970s there were stories that engine 49 was chosen to be refurbished and once again used, this time to haul tourists, but that plan was quickly shot down after a few trial trips. No one would say why, but engine 49 was subsequently sold to a private collector.

The collector took it to Bedford, Pennsylvania, where he began to gather parts to restore the train. The engine's whistle had been removed and sold separately, and the collector went to great pains to find it. After he reunited the whistle and engine, he began to see a mist in the engine. The first time it happened he thought it was an illusion, but time and again the mist appeared. Then the whistle began going off despite the fact that no one was in the engine. The collector removed the whistle once more.

He became apprehensive of the engine after researching it and realizing that three men had died because of that engine. He had the engine hauled to a field where it could harm no one. There engine 49 sat for years. It rusted and became derelict, but people insisted that they saw mist around the engine.

The collector finally put the engine up for sale, and for now its location is unknown. In time, though, someone will decide to restore the Ghost and put it back to use carrying tourists or private patrons. Sadly, they might not know about the curse until it claims another life.

27

THE PHANTOM
HANDPRINT

The mining of coal in Pennsylvania has been both a blessing and a curse. Once the bread-and-butter industry of the Commonwealth, extraction of this solid, black, transportable energy source made poor men rich and rich men richer. But along with the work came the lethal danger and monetary exploitation of human labor.

William Penn knew about the possibility of coal in his "woods" in 1698. Coal was first noted on a map in 1753; in 1754 George Washington's expedition reported that they had seen coal in the area they were surveying; in 1761 there was a coal mine at Fort Pitt near the site that would later become Pittsburgh.

Coal was also discovered in northeastern Pennsylvania, and mining near Pittston began in 1775. Seventeen years later, the Lehigh Coal Mining Company was shipping coal to Philadelphia.

In the late eighteenth century, coal fired the Industrial Revolution throughout the world. The miracle of machines doing the work of transporting goods and people had the potential to free both humans and animals of backbreaking work, and it increased output to benefit the masses. Steam engines were moving vehicles across land and water and powering sawmills to render timber into lumber to build structures.

Coal began to be used for heating and cooking in homes both large and small, and various adjunct industries sprouted. To transport the coal via water, canals were constructed with their locks, dams, boats, and canal-side inns, and people were employed to build and manage them. Blacksmiths, bakers, and brewers found coal the ideal source of heat for their trades. Railroads soon came along and used the coal for power to move more coal to consumers around the Commonwealth and into neighboring states.

But along with the progress and the profits came the danger inherent in mining coal. The deeper the workers had to go for the coal, the more commonplace cave-ins and shaft collapses became. Miners were killed and maimed. Coal dust explosions literally tore men apart as violently as any weapon produced in wartime. It wasn't until after years in the mines that coal miners would begin to cough and the horror of breathing in coal dust for a lifetime was named: black lung disease.

Fourteen-hour workdays were often expected of the men. Stores in the remote regions of coal mines were owned by the coal companies and charged exorbitant prices for essentials, which low miners' wages could not cover. Expensive company-owned housing also took the miners' meager pay at a steady, monthly rate. Deeper in debt they descended until they were unable to escape. One story has it that if a miner was killed in the mine, by evening his body would be dumped unceremoniously on his widow's front porch, a notice that she and her children must vacate the company's house posthaste.

Worst of all, children became employees of the mining companies at a young age as "breaker boys," able to squeeze into areas full-grown men could not go to extract the last bits of the black rock. So generation after generation became entrapped.

Eventually the new wave of organizing workers into unions made its way into the industry, but not without resistance from the coal companies and their owners. No social movement in America has been as bitter, or as deadly, as the unionization of the mining industry. And no group was more well known for its violence than the Molly Maguires.

The name came from an organization in Ireland in the 1840s that fought against the tyranny of unscrupulous landlords. It came to America as a secret society in 1862. In July 1863, a few days after the Battle of Gettysburg, the Molly Maguires were involved in street riots in Philadelphia, ostensibly to protest the national military draft instituted to fill the ever-depleting ranks of the Federal army. The riots soon turned violent, ugly, and racial, with rioters lynching African Americans on lampposts and burning their bodies.

After the Civil War the Mollies turned their attention to the coal mines. Their strategy was not to negotiate, but to intimidate mine bosses, owners, management, and even local judges and police by physical threats, strikes, and violence. Their goals were to force the mines to provide decent wages and better working conditions. To achieve their goals, they were not above committing murder.

Their tactics involved terror. They delivered to their targets "coffin notices," which consisted of a note indicating the violence about to be perpetrated upon the recipient should he not follow the Mollies' demands, and a coffin, replete with skull and crossbones and rosary beads drawn upon it. They often imported Mollies from other areas of Pennsylvania to do their violence, then vanish. Favors were remembered and returned. Every Molly seemed to have an airtight alibi for the time of the crime.

The crimes were heinous and began nearly as soon as the Molly Maguires were instituted in the United States.

In 1862 mine foreman Frank W. J. Langdon was stoned to death. Though the crime was connected to the Mollies, all those accused had an alibi. Our the next six years several more murders were committed and blamed on the Mollies. Then, in 1872, mine boss Morgan Powell was killed.

More cold-blooded killings occurred in the coal region of northeastern Pennsylvania. Tamaqua policeman Frank B. Yost was attending to his duties, extinguishing street lamps from a ladder, when he was shot in the back on July 6, 1875. In September, in Raven Run, Thomas Sanger was on his way to work at Heaton's Colliery with a man named Uren whom he had hired as a bodyguard. A Molly Maguire named "Friday" O'Donnell came up to them, pulled a gun, and shot them both. Sanger was wounded in the arm and ran back to his home. Another Molly blocked his way. When he turned to run he stumbled, and a third Molly, identified as Thomas Munley, shot him where he lay. To make sure Sanger was dead, another man rolled him over and shot him again.

To "celebrate," the men ran to the nearest bar. Munley shouted to what he thought was a sympathetic crowd, "I shot the first man as he was trying to get into a house." At least one patron of the bar, however, was far from sympathetic.

In 1874 the mine owners had solicited the services of Allan Pinkerton, founder of the famous Pinkerton Detective Agency, which had protected Abraham Lincoln during the Civil War. His men had infiltrated the Mollies and their home turf. One of Pinkerton's detectives was sitting in the very bar where Munley shot off his mouth.

But Pinkerton could not move fast enough to protect John P. Jones, who was attacked just two days later, on September 3, 1875. Jones had received the infamous coffin notices and began arming himself when he left the house for work at night. During the day, however, he felt secure enough to leave his weapon at home. Surely no one would commit murder in broad daylight.

He underestimated the moxie of the Mollies, emboldened, perhaps, by the murder of Sanger. Jones was only five minutes from his home when he was shot in the back. He was able to run at first but then collapsed in some bushes. A number of men followed him and pumped bullets into him as he writhed, defenseless. One of the assailants was named Jimmy Kerrigan.

Finally, the backlash came. Suspects were rounded up. Trials were scheduled. Jimmy Kerrigan, fearful for his own life, turned on his fellow Mollies. His testimony, along with that of the Pinkerton agent, sealed the fate of several Molly Maguires, convicted for the premeditated murders of police and mine bosses.

Convictions came quickly. Dates for executions were set. Six were to be hanged in Pottsville, four in the Carbon County jail in Mauch Chunk (now named Jim Thorpe), on June 21, 1877. Justice would indeed be swift. At least nine more would swing from the gallows in 1878.

The dragnet was not only swift but perhaps even hasty. Sometimes just being named as a Molly was enough to land one in jail. Often, just being Irish was enough for suspicion and arrest. So it appeared with Alexander Campbell.

Campbell had emigrated from Ireland in 1868, settling in Tamaqua and opening a tavern. After moving to Carbon County he joined a fraternal organization, the Ancient Order of Hibernians, and through that got involved with the Molly Maguires. Their terroristic tactics intimidated a lot of people but not the sheriff of Carbon County. Ten men were caught up in his sweep for justice for the murder of Morgan Powell, among others. Alexander Campbell was one of them, protesting his innocence all the way to his jail cell—and beyond.

Try as they might, the Mollies failed in their efforts to intimidate the county judge . The ten men were tried and sentenced to hang by the neck until dead. One was confident he would walk. He told others he had helped get Pennsylvania governor John Hartranft elected by delivering the Irish vote to him. Imagine his surprise when, as he stood with the noose around his neck, his commutation failed to arrive.

Campbell protested his innocence, saying he wasn't anywhere near the site of the murders when they occurred. Indeed, he didn't seem like your regular Molly Maguire ruffian. He had been a delegate to a local democratic convention and was considered well-to-do. A local newspaper announced that a ball was to be sponsored by Alexander Campbell and a fine time was expected to be had by all. After his trial he was convinced that the Commonwealth would reverse the conviction since everyone knew the witnesses perjured themselves in their testimony. Local residents served as character witnesses, testifying to the pardons board of Campbell's upstanding personality. Campbell's defense attorney wrote to the same board, stating that "the character of the material witnesses against him, was so palpably infamous, and the game they played so certainly in the interest of their own forfeited necks, that I could not agree to a verdict that would take Campbell's life—nor can I now."

To be fair, the Irish in nineteenth-century America were savagely discriminated against, and Campbell—caught up in the era with its cruel working conditions, the workers' struggle for a safe workplace and fair wages, and the general anti-Irish prejudice—became, rightly or wrongly, a victim. Further historical research has indicated that several of the other Mollies hanged were in the process of involving themselves in local politics in order to legitimately help the plight of the persecuted and downtrodden in their communities, their potential rise to power perhaps a threat to the powers that be. They, as well, may have been innocent and railroaded by a system stacked against them.

Alexander Campbell, however, took proof of his innocence literally in his own hands, and to a higher, otherworldly power.

Throughout his incarceration in Mauch Chunk jail cell number 17, Campbell maintained his blamelessness. He claimed he was nowhere near where the murders had been committed. But, of course, that alibi had been used time and time again by the Mollies.

June 21, 1877, was set as the day of execution. Ever since it has been known as "the Day of the Rope." Contemporary reports seemed to give it a holiday feel—to everyone, of course, but the ten men condemned to take their last breaths that day.

Six were to die in Pottsville for the murder of Frank Yost, the policeman who was simply doing his duty. In Mauch Chunk, at eight thirty in the morning, the Easton Grays, a local militia unit, marched with loaded weapons to guard the jail where the executions would take place. The gallows had been constructed in the corridor of the building. Every hammer blow and saw cut was heard by the condemned during the construction.

A little after ten thirty the four doomed men, including Alexander Campbell, were paraded from their cells and up the thirteen steps to stand over the trapdoor. Each was accompanied by a priest and carried a crucifix. They saw the last of this world as hoods were placed over their heads. At 10:48 a.m. the trapdoor was released and their drop to the jail floor was stopped short by the rough hemp nooses about their necks.

Two of the condemned struggled at the end of their ropes in a hideous death dance. In an effort to relieve suffering, a priest massaged holy oil on one of the dying men's hands. It relieved nothing.

Alexander Campbell did not struggle, but his was the last heart to stop beating, fourteen minutes after the trap was sprung. It was one of the ways he managed to proclaim his reluctance to die a guilty man.

The other way he managed to protest his innocence is still in evidence to this day.

As the hangman opened the door to cell 17 to lead Campbell on his one-way trip through the jail, Campbell placed his hand on the cell wall and vowed his handprint would remain as long as the jail stood, a sign that the Commonwealth of Pennsylvania had murdered an innocent man.

To the chagrin of the next occupant of cell 17, the print would not, no matter how hard he tried, rub off the cell wall. The jailer would try to erase the strange mark as well, to no avail. That jailer and subsequent employees of the jail would scrub in vain at the mark of an apparently innocent man and, in fact, paint over it, only to have the eerie evidence reappear. Finally, a sheriff by the name of Beigler, tired of the notoriety the mysterious mark was giving his jail, had the wall torn down and a new one rebuilt.

Alexander Campbell apparently revisited his old cell, for soon after the print returned.

In the 1960s Sheriff Charles Neast slathered a thick coat of green latex paint to cover the print once and for all. In a short while Campbell's handprint was back.

More recently James Starrs, renowned forensic scientist at George Washington University, and Jeff Kercheval, a police chemist from Hagerstown, Maryland, examined the print with high-tech equipment at their disposal. "There's no logical explanation for it" was Starrs's conclusion.

SELECT BIBLIOGRAPHY

"About Centralia PA and the Mine Fire." www.centraliapa.org/about -centralia-pa-mine-fire.

Andrelczyk, Mike. "A Mysterious Hex: Murder at Rehmeyer Hollow." *Fly*, October 3, 2014. www.Flymagazine.net/mysterious-hex-murder -rehmeyer-hollow.

"Chickies Rock County Park." Lancaster County, Pennsylvania. web .co.lancaster.pa.us/262/Chickies-Rock-County-Park.

Clark, Dennis. *The Irish in Philadelphia.* Philadelphia: Temple UP, 1973.

Davis, Burke. *They Called Him Stonewall: A Life of Lieutenant General T. J. Jackson.* New York: Fairfax Press, 1988.

Duffy's Cut Project website. www.duffyscutproject.com.

Egerton, Douglas R. *Gabriel's Rebellion: The Virginia Slave Conspiracies of 1800 and 1802.* Chapel Hill: University of North Carolina Press, 1993.

Execution of Molly Maguires (historical marker). Explore PA History. www.explorepahistory.com/hmarker.php?markerId=1-A-3B9.

Fisher, Rick. *Ghosts of the River Towns.* Marietta, PA: Fisher Productions, 2006.

Flaherty Anne. "Alex Campbell's Wake." *From John Kehoe's Cell* blog, October 15, 2011. www.mythofmollymaguires.blogspot.com/2011/10/ alex-campbells-wake_15.html

Frassanito, William A. *Gettysburg: A Journey in Time.* New York: Charles Scribner's Sons, 1975.

Gates, G. Thomas. "The Blue-Eyed Six." In *A History of Hangings for Homicide in Lebanon County*. Lebanon, PA: Lebanon County Historical Society, 1971.

"Hawk Mountain." Tri-County Paranormal Research. www.delcoghosts .com/hawk_mountain.html.

Heffernan, Tim, and Graeme Wood. "The Wrong Box." *National Review*, April 20, 2015.

Hoover, Stephanie. "Superstitious Dauphin County Residents Shun 'Witch.'" Hauntingly Pennsylvania. www.hauntinglypa.com/ dauphin_county_residents_shun_witch.html.

Huesken Jr., Gerald. "The Strange Case of Hawk Mountain and Matthias Schambacher." Examiner.com, October 26, 2010. www .examiner.com/article/the-strange-case-of-hawk-mountain-and -matthias-schambacher.

Ieraci, Ron. "Moonshine Church & Cemetery." *Pennsylvania Haunts & History* blog, August 2008. www.hauntsandhistory.blogspot.com/ 2008/08/moonshine-church-cemetery.html.

———. "Pennsylvania Dutch Haunts and History." Pennsylvania Haunts & History. https://sites.google.com/site/hauntsandhistory/ pennsylvaniadutchhaunts%26history.

Kraut, Alan M. *Silent Travelers: Germs, Genes, and the "Immigrant Menace."* Baltimore: Johns Hopkins UP, 1994.

Lake, Matt. *Weird Pennsylvania*. New York: Sterling, 2007.

Langan, Sheila. "Irish Woman Murdered at Duffy's Cut in 1832 Begins Journey Home." IrishCentral, May 9, 2015. www.irishcentral .com/roots/history/Journey-home-begins-at-last-for-Irish-woman -murdered-at-Duffys-Cut-in-1832-.html.

Linebaugh, Peter. "The Day of the Rope." *Counterpunch*, June 21, 2007. www.counterpunch.org/2007/06/21/the-day-of-the-rope.

Martin, Brandy M. Watts. "Rausch Gap." StonyValley.com. http://stonyvalley.com/rauschgap.htm.

McPherson, James. *Battle Cry of Freedom: The Civil War Era*. New York: Oxford UP, 1988.

Nesbitt, Mark. *Ghosts of Gettysburg: Spirits, Apparitions and Haunted Places of the Battlefield*. 7 vols. Gettysburg, PA: Second Chance Publications, 1991–2011.

Nesbitt, Mark, and Patty A. Wilson. *The Big Book of Pennsylvania Ghost Stories*. Mechanicsburg, PA: Stackpole Books, 2008.

———. *Haunted Pennsylvania: Ghosts and Strange Phenomena of the Keystone State*. Mechanicsburg, PA: Stackpole Books, 2006.

Oakes, Amy. "Tavern Owner's Legend Still Haunts Hawk Mountain. Some Believe Matthias Schaumboch Lured Weary Travelers, Murdered Them." *The Morning Call* (Lehigh Valley, PA), March 16, 1997. http://articles.mcall.com/1997-03-16/news/3128317_1_hawk-mountain-sanctuary-association-stories-ghost.

Oates, Stephen B. *The Fires of Jubilee: Nat Turner's Fierce Rebellion*. New York: New American Library, 1975.

"Pa. Germans' Beliefs in Witchcraft Subject of Book." *Lebanon Daily News*, [date].

Patterson, Gerard A. "The Death of Iverson's Brigade." Gettysburg Discussion Group. www.gdg.org/Gettysburg%20Magazine/iverson.html.

Pullen, John J. *The 20th Maine*. Greenwich, CT: Fawcett, 1962.

Schreiwer, Robert Lusch. "Ewicher Yeeger." *Deitsch Mythology* blog, November 24, 2013. http://deitschmythology.blogspot.com/2013/11/ewicher-yeeger.html.

Small, Cindy L. *The Jennie Wade Story: A True and Complete Account of the Only Civilian Killed During the Battle of Gettysburg.* Gettysburg, PA: Thomas Publications, 1991.

Smith, Norman A. "Der Alt Hexa Zehner" (in German). *The Pennsylvania Dutchman* 1, no. 17 (August 25, 1949).

Tucker, Glenn. *High Tide at Gettysburg: The Campaign in Pennsylvania.* Indianapolis: Bobbs-Merrill, 1958.

Uruburu, Paula. *American Eve.* New York: Riverhead Books, 2008.

Valania, Jonathan. "Murder in the Time of Cholera." *Philadelphia Weekly*, August 17, 2010. www.philadelphiaweekly.com/news-and-opinion/cover-story/Murder-in-the-Time-of-Cholera.html.

Watson, William E., J. Francis Watson, John H. Ahtes III, and Earl H. Schandelmeier III. *The Ghosts of Duffy's Cut: The Irish Who Died Building America's Most Dangerous Stretch of Railroad.* New York: Praeger, 2006.

Wilson, Patty A. *Haunted Pennsylvania.* Laceyville, PA: Belfry Books, 1998.

———. *The Pennsylvania Ghost Guide.* Vol. 2. Roaring Spring, PA: Piney Creek Press, 2001.

Yoder, Don, ed. "A Legend of Alle-Maengel." *The Pennsylvania Dutchman* 1, no. 12 (July 21, 1949).

INDEX

C

camera malfunctions, 31–32
Campbell, Alexander, 186–89
Capone, Al, 165–71
Carlisle, Pennsylvania, 17, 40
carriage industry, 37–38
cars, 173–77
Casey, Bob, 73
cats, 141, 142
cemeteries, 21, 174–77
Centralia, Pennsylvania, 71–73
chairs
   curse-maker identification
     using, 118–20
   entities knocking over, 163
   prisoner mistreatment and
     "mad," 168
Chamberlain, Joshua L., 3
Chambersburg, Pennsylvania,
   12–13, 40
Chancellorsville, Battle of, 18, 39
Charles II, King of England, ix
Chet (father of cursed baby), 115,
   119, 120, 123
Chickies Rock County Park,
   67–70
children
   baby curses, 115–23
   child abuse, 144–46, 150
   hauntings in bedrooms of,
     141–50
   mining and labor of, 184
   Native American attacks, 99
cholera epidemics, 45–49
Christianity
   Bible as resource for curse-
     breaking incantations, 91

Bible as witchcraft resource,
   104
   himmelbriefs with Bible
     verses, 105
   prayers for curse-breaking
     incantations, 120, 121, 123
   prayers for protection, 126–27
   on witchcraft, 92–93
Civil War. *See also* Battle of
   Gettysburg
   battlefield photographs of, 31,
     33–35
   battles of, 18, 26, 38–39
   Confederate regiments, 17–23,
     38–39
   death statistics, 15–16
   draft riots, 184–85
   ghosts of, 1–3, 22–23
   leadership protocols, 19
   in Pennsylvania, xi
Clark, James, 169–70
cleansing rituals, 80–81, 122–23,
   133
coal mining
   child labor, 184
   health issues, 184
   industry development, xi–xii,
     183–84
   tragedies and miner deaths,
     184
   train collisions, 57–59
   underground fires, 71–73
   unionization and activist
     violence, 184–89
   work conditions and housing,
     184
Coddington, John, 72

Fort Pitt, 183
Fox, George, ix
Frank (son of Jesse), 132–38,
    138–39
Franklin, Benjamin, xii, 166
Frassanito, William A., 33–35
Fredericksburg, Battle of, 26, 39
French and Indian War, x
Fugitive Slave Act, 7, 11
Fulton County, Pennsylvania, 141

G
Gabriel's Rebellion, 8
Gail (wife/mother), 141–50
gangsters, 165–66, 169–70
Gardner, Alexander, 31, 34–35
Gerhardt, Jacob, 99–100
German (Deutsch) settlers, 51–55
Germantown, Battle of, x, 83
Gettysburg. *See also* Battle of
    Gettysburg
  culture and language, 37
  Native American history at,
    27–29
  postwar presidential addresses
    in, xi
  prewar industries in, 37–38
  site descriptions, 25
  visitor experiences and
    descriptions, 29
Gettysburg: Journey in Time, A
    (Frassanito), 34–35
Ghost, the (train engine), 179–82
ghosts
  of abolitionists, 16
  black shadow people, 125–29,
    141–50, 170

at Chickies Rock, 67–68
destructive, 76–81
at Eastern State Penitentiary,
    169–71
at Elmhurst estate, 161–63
of eternal hunters, 51–55
of executed military aides, 88
of farmers, 67–68
of gangsters, 169–70
Gettysburg battlefield, 1–3,
    22–23, 31–33, 35
immigrant workers at Duffy's
    Cut, 47–49
of inns, 102
intelligent/interactive, 69
at John Brown's Tannery, 16
men struck by trains, 69
of military horsemen, 1, 2–3,
    22, 89
of murdered brauchers, 106
of murdered elderly women,
    137–39
Native American, 27, 28
paranormal theory of, 16
railroader's widows, 58–59
of rebellious slaves, 9
at Ritner Boarding House, 16
robbers, 69
women in white, 1–2
of World War II veterans,
    110–13
Ghosts of Gettysburg (Nesbitt), 1, 22
Gibson, Charles Dana, 153
Gibson Girls, 153
Gilday, Emma, 91–98
Gilday, Mrs., 93–94, 96
Gilday, William, 91–98

Girl in the Red Velvet Swing. *See*
 Nesbit, Florence Evelyn
Girl in the Red Velvet Swing, The
 (movie), 161
goatmen, 75–81
graves, mass, 46–49
greed, 61–66
green glows, 47
Green Tree Tavern, 47
growling, 76, 78
guilt, 57–59
Gusenberg, Frank, 166

H

Haitian curses, 78–81
Hall, Charles, xii
halos, 138
Hamtramck Guards, 38
handprints, 77, 189
Hanover, Pennsylvania, 2, 40
Harpers Ferry, Virginia, 12,
 13–14
Hartranft, John, 187
hate, 75–81, 145, 150
Haviland, John, 167
Hawk Mountain, 99–102
Hawk Mountain Raptor
 Sanctuary, 99, 102
headless horsemen, 1
Helen (mother of cursed baby),
 115–23
Hell on Earth, 71–73
Hess, Wilbert, 105–6
Hetty (grandmother), 145–46
hexeria (witchcraft)
 accusations and executions,
 104

African, 108, 109–13
 baby curses, 115–23
 Haitian spells, 78–81
 hex signs, 103
 practitioners of, 91, 95–98,
 103–6, 113
 references for, 104
 spells and reversal rituals,
 91–98
 word definition, 103
Hex Hollow, 104–5
hex signs, 103
himmelbriefs, 105
hissing, 93–98
Hohman, Johann Georg, 104
horsemen ghosts, 1, 2–3, 22, 89
hounds, 51–55
houses
 appearances/disappearances
 of, 69
 haunted, 141–50
 interior destruction of, 76–77
 purification rituals for, 81,
 122–23
Howe, Sir William, x–xi
humanoid creatures, 69–70
hunters
 eternal, 51–55
 Native American ghosts
 guiding lost, 27

I

ice baths, 168
Igbo tribespeople, 8–9
immigrants
 African slaves, 5–10
 German (Deutsch), 51–55

Nesbit, Florence Evelyn (Girl in the Red Velvet Swing)
  birth and childhood, 151–52
  death, 161
  divorce, 161
  ghost of, 162–63
  health issues, 156, 158
  later years, 161
  modeling jobs, 152, 153
  movies about, 161
  murder trials, 160
  pregnancy, 161
  relationships and marriages, 153–59
  theatrical career, 153, 161
Nesbit, Mrs. (mother), 151–52, 154, 156, 157
Nesbitt, Mark
  camera malfunctions, 31–33
  ghost encounters, 1
  ghost story publications, 1, 22
  Native American ghost stories, 27
New Jersey (battleship), xii
Nigerian slaves, 8–9
noises
  battlefield, 22
  dishes crashing, 142
  dogs baying, 53–55
  footsteps, 161, 162, 170
  growling, 76, 78
  knife sharpening, 102
  laughter, 170
  pounding, 111, 112, 150, 161
  screaming/wailing, 23, 101, 102, 134, 170
  train whistles, 181, 182
  tribal drumming, 68

voices, 22–23, 161–62, 170, 171
whispering, 170
Noll, Nellie, 105
Northwest Indian War, 85–86

O

O'Donnell, "Friday," 185
O'Sullivan, Timothy, 31, 34–35

P

pain, 115–23, 150
Paoli, Battle of, 83
papers, legal, 79–81
Peaches (cat), 141, 142
Peach Orchard (Gettysburg), 42
Peggy (babysitter/missionary), 125–29
penitentiaries, 166–69
Penn, William, Jr., ix–x, 183
Penn, William, Sr., ix
Pennsylvania, overview
  agricultural history, xii
  early settlers, 51–55
  forest fires, 5
  founding of, ix
  industry and economic development, xi–xii
  military history, x–xi
  nicknames for, x, xii
  slavery abolition, 7–8
Pennsylvania Dutch culture
  folk medicine practices, 103–6
  ill-gotten gains and earthbound spirits beliefs, 69
  language and sayings, 37
  supernatural creatures, 69–70

purification rituals, 80–81,
122–23, 133
Puttstown, Pennsylvania, 131
pyramids, 28–29

Q

Quakers, ix, x, 7, 166–67

R

racism, 75–81. *See also* slaves and
slavery
Rae, Alexander, 71
Rail City, 181
railroad engineers, 58, 71, 179,
180–81
railroads
immigrant worker deaths,
45–49
individuals struck by trains,
69
industry development, xi–xii
suicides by train, 58–59
train collisions and passenger
deaths, 57–58
train engines cursed, 179–82
train tracks, categories of, 179
railways, electric, 67
rape, 157
Rausch Gap, 57–59
reasons for curses
discontentment, 31–35, 51–55,
109–13
greed, 61–66
guilt, 57–59
murder and injustice, 45–49,
83–89
murder and loss of love,
67–68

overview, vii
racism and hatred, 75–81
revenge, 68–69, 71–73, 91–98
spirit possession, 99–102,
141–50
spitefulness, 120
wartime trauma, 1–3, 22–23,
27–29
rebellions, 8, 10–15, 184–85
Rehmeyer, Nelson, 105–6
Religious Society of Friends, ix
Rendell, Ed, 73
repentance, as penal system
concept, 166–69
revenge, as reason for curse,
68–69, 71–73, 91–98
revolts, 8, 10–15, 184–85
Riley, Jonathan, 75–76
riots, 8, 10–15, 184–85
Riter, Joseph, 12
Ritner Boarding House, 12–13, 16
robbers, 69
Rock, Reuben, 107–13
Rose Farm, 34
Ryan (possessed husband/
father), 141–50

S

Sachar, Louis, vii
Sach's Covered Bridge, 39
Salem witch trials, 104
salt, for purification rituals, 81,
122–23, 133
Sanger, Thomas, 185
Sarah (psychic woman), 131–39
Satan, 61–66, 88, 125–29
sausages, 100
Saxton, Pennsylvania, 131

unions, labor, 184
unrequited love, 67–68, 91–98
Uren (bodyguard), 185

V

Valania, Jonathan, 47
Valley Forge, xi, 83
Vesey, Denmark, 9
voices, 22–23, 161–62, 170, 171
voodoo, 108, 109–13

W

Wade, Mary Virginia "Jenny," 43
wailing, 102
Wanhuita (Native American
     woman), 67–68
Wanunga (Native American
     man), 67–68
wars. *See also* Battle of
     Gettysburg; Civil War
     American Revolution, x–xi,
          83–85
     French and Indian War, x
     Northwest Indian War, 85–86
     tribal, 27–29
     World War II, xii, 107–8
war whoops, 28
Washington, George
     expedition surveys and coal,
          183
     ghost of, 2–3
     military service, x–xi, 83–84,
          85
Watson, Bill, 46–49
Watson, Frank, 46, 47–49
Wayne, Anthony, 83–89
Wayne, Isaac, 88–89

Wheatfield (Gettysburg), 42
whispering, 170
whistles, train, 181, 182
White, Stanford, 153–54, 155,
     157, 159
widows, 57–59
Wills, David, 21
Wilson, Patty, 22–23, 75–81
Winchester, Battle of, 26
Wisconsin (battleship), xii
witchcraft (hexeria)
     accusations and executions,
          104
     African, 108, 109–13
     baby curses, 115–23
     Haitian spells, 78–81
     hex signs, 103
     land curses, 68–69
     practitioners of, 91, 95–98,
          103–6, 113
     references for, 104
     spells and reversal rituals,
          91–98
wives
     farmers', 61–66
     railroader's widows, 57–59
Wolf, Dr., 95–96
Woman in White (ghost), 1–2
World War II, xii, 107–8

Y

Yeeger, Ewicher, 51–55
Yost, Frank B., 185, 188

Z

Zook, Jakob, 103
zoot suit-dressed figures, 125–29

ABOUT THE AUTHORS

Mark Nesbitt was a National Park Service ranger/historian for five years at Gettysburg before starting his own research and writing company. Since then he has published fourteen books, including the national award–winning *Ghosts of Gettysburg* series. His stories have been seen on the History Channel, A&E, the Discovery Channel, the Travel Channel, *Unsolved Mysteries,* and numerous regional television shows and heard on Coast to Coast AM and regional radio. In 1994 Nesbitt created the commercially successful Ghosts of Gettysburg Candlelight Walking Tours and in 2006, the Ghosts of Fredericksburg Tours.

Patty A. Wilson lives in central Pennsylvania with her three sons. She has been a writer for thirty years and has nineteen books to her credit. She has written about diverse subjects, including Pennsylvania, West Virginia, and North Carolina folklore, the paranormal, farming, cooking, and history. She has appeared as an expert on various television shows, including *Mysterious Journeys* and *My Ghost Story.* Wilson enjoys people and loves working as a lecturer and tour guide in central Pennsylvania. She hosts a blog on Examiner.com and created the Ghost Research Foundation (www.ghostsrus.com). She truly enjoys discovering and sharing the more colorful side of history and the paranormal. Follow her on Twitter at @ghostladyofpa.